UNLOCK
AI MASTERY

Secrets to Accelerate Business Growth and Dominate
Competitors with Proven AI Strategies

Nikky Kho and Nikhal Ghai

DISCLAIMER AND/OR LEGAL NOTICES

While all attempts have been made to verify information provided in this book and its ancillary materials, neither the author or publisher assumes any responsibility for errors, inaccuracies or omissions and is not responsible for any financial loss by customer in any manner. Any slights of people or organizations are unintentional. If advice concerning legal, financial, accounting, or related matters is needed, the services of a qualified professional should be sought. This book and its associated ancillary materials, including verbal and written training, is not intended for use as a source of legal, financial, or accounting advice. You should be aware of the various laws governing business transactions or other business practices in your particular geographical location.

EARNINGS & INCOME DISCLAIMER

With respect to the reliability, accuracy, timeliness, usefulness, adequacy, completeness, and/or suitability of the information provided in this book, Nicholas Kho, Nikhal Ghai, Real AI Dynamics, Inc., its partners, associates, affiliates, consultants, and/or presenters make no warranties, guarantees, representations, or claims of any kind.

Readers' results will vary depending on a number of factors. Any and all claims or representations regarding income earnings should not be considered average earnings. Testimonials are not representative. This book, along with its products and services, is intended solely for educational and informational purposes.

Important Notes:

- AI was utilized in producing some content in this book.
- Use caution and consult with qualified professionals, such as accountants, attorneys, or advisors, before acting on any information presented here.
- You agree that Nikhal Ghai, Nicholas Kho, and Real AI Dynamics, Inc. are not responsible for the success or failure of your personal, business, health, or financial decisions based on this information.

Earnings potential is entirely dependent on individual efforts, skills, and application. Any examples, stories, references, or case studies are purely illustrative and should not be interpreted as typical results or guarantees. No part of this material promises actual performance or guarantees success.

The information, strategies, concepts, techniques, exercises, and ideas presented in this book and related materials are based on personal opinions and experiences. They should not be misinterpreted as assurances or guarantees of specific outcomes (expressed or implied).

The author and publisher (Nikhal Ghai, Nicholas Kho, Real AI Dynamics, Inc. (RAID), or any representatives of RAID) shall not be held liable under any circumstances for any direct, indirect, punitive, special, incidental, or consequential damages arising from the use of books, materials, and/or seminar trainings. All information is provided "as is," without warranties of any kind.

DEDICATION

To our family and friends, whose unwavering support and love have been our greatest strength; to the incredible team at Real AI Dynamics (RAID), thank you for your dedication and collaboration in shaping the future of AI; and to the entire AI community, your innovation and passion inspire us every day. This book is a reflection of all the shared knowledge, experiences, and progress we've made together. We couldn't have done it without you.

— Nikhal Ghai & Nikky Kho

My love for my parents, brother, and the rest of my family that have provided so much support for me throughout my life.

— Nikky Kho

Foreword

Welcome to *Real AI Dynamics: Mastering AI for Business Success*! In this book, we delve into the transformative power of AI, demystifying its complexities and breaking down its foundational principles. Whether you are just starting to explore AI or looking to refine your understanding, this book offers a comprehensive guide to the basics of AI, practical use cases across various industries, and actionable insights. With simplified workflows and easy-to-understand concepts, we aim to empower you to incorporate AI seamlessly into your operations, helping you drive efficiency, innovation, and success.

At Real AI Dynamics, we believe AI is not just for the tech-savvy; it's a tool that anyone can harness to scale their business, streamline processes, and solve real-world problems. This book provides tips, tricks, and strategies for leveraging AI effectively, helping you stay ahead in today's competitive landscape. Our goal is to make AI accessible to all, offering clear and practical solutions to integrate AI into your business strategies with confidence and ease.

Enjoy the journey!

Nikhal Ghai and Nikky Kho

Testimonials

"Nicholas Kho took a simple idea to the extreme. He gathered a mastermind. Kho branded his as the gold standard of the industry."

"Many of us successful entrepreneurs laugh our way to the bank as people scratch their heads, trying to figure out how. Kho started this company after traveling around the world. He became really good at helping others succeed as he did. Nicholas Kho took a simple idea to the extreme. He gathered a Mastermind. Kho branded his as the gold standard of the industry. He had no doubt this program would be successful, since he got such amazing results from it himself. And it was!"

Nick Friedman

Producer, Best-Selling Author, Star of the Hit TV Show "Shark Tank," Inc. 5000 CEO of College H.U.N.K.S. Hauling Junk, $200+ Million in Annual Revenue, EY Entrepreneur of the Year

"I have applied what Nick teaches in both my personal and business life, and the results have been transformative."

"The workshop is fantastic, and I have successfully used his methods to engage people in the downtown project in Vegas. Nick is not only a great friend but also someone I trust deeply. He and his team have been advising our company on corporate culture, and we've had a lot of fun working together."

"One of my personal goals was to be able to go to any city where nobody knows me and use the tools Nick teaches about social dynamics and high-status communication, without any preconceived notions about how I should be treated. Thanks to Nick, I now have the confidence and skills to achieve this."

Tony Hsieh

Founder and CEO of Zappos from Las Vegas

Anthony Hsieh was an American internet entrepreneur and venture capitalist. He retired as the CEO of the online shoe and clothing company Zappos in August 2020 after 21 years. Prior to joining Zappos, Hsieh co-founded the Internet advertising network LinkExchange.

"It's rare to work with someone who not only has a vast amount of knowledge and passion for business but also has the leadership and patience to mentor those who work with him."

"I had the pleasure of working with Nick as his business manager. Nick's work ethic is second to none, and his ability to combine work ethic and strategic decision-making creates an innovative efficiency that I have not seen since working with him. Nick's entrepreneurial spirit is contagious and motivates those who work with him to achieve goals they do not believe they can achieve. Nick's never-ending drive for excellence raises the standard of quality for all that work with him. Lastly, Nick's social networking abilities are phenomenal. Nick has a combination of charisma and benevolence that leads to genuine, long-term relationships with anyone who he meets him."

Noah St. John

PhD, Bestselling Author, Executive Coach, & Contributor at Entrepreneur Media from Ohio

"Nikky Kho, we love you and you are a rockstar. Keep up the fantastic work!"

"Thank you, Nikky! Our team left the presentation inspired and educated… and with their mind blown. Mission accomplished! Really appreciate it!"

Aditya Paul Berlia

Founder of Vjal Institute from Dubai

"Thanks again for the fabulous presentation today. You provided helpful information that I hope the coaches take advantage of."

"Content providers have never had more powerful tools at their disposal than they do with AI."

"Great stuff, great job!"

Gary Chappell

CEO of Nightingale-Conant from Chicago, Illinois, USA

"Nick is one of the smartest and most brilliant people I know. His expertise in AI is unmatched, and he has an incredible ability to share his knowledge in ways that are both practical and inspiring.

Nick's curiosity and endless appetite for learning have made him a wise teacher and an exceptional leader, benefiting so many. His even temperament and humility make him not only a trusted mentor but also a great friend. I look forward to the day when the Guinness Book of World Records recognizes him for the remarkable degrees and achievements he's earned."

Perry Belcher

Co-Founder of Digital Marketer from Las Vegas

Perry Belcher has seen and done it all in the business world. From sales to web promotion to consulting and venture capital projects, Perry has been involved in many lucrative businesses over the years.

"Nick is a Rock Star, traveling around the world and making things happen. I know this guy cares. He works his tail off to serve, create, and add more value. It is not once in awhile, it is consistently. I think that is the sign of a great entrepreneur. Do the things that people would never do to get the things in their life that most people will never have. I want you to keep up the good work. What you are doing is pretty awesome! Life is really about being shown those opportunities and it's about what you do with them. To me that is the difference. The difference maker for those that really make it happen is they don't wonder what happen, they make it happen. That's what this guy helps you do. Their team is awesome. I met a lot of their trainers, a lot of their coaches, and they live it every day."

Bill Walsh

CEO of PowerTeam International from Chicago

"Nick is the leader of a bunch of influencers with really nice big, huge social media followings and they all have courses, but under one company. Kinda like the Wu Tang Clan or a franchise. It's really interesting. They don't spend money on Facebook or YouTube. It's mostly social media. He doesn't just have one guy. He has an army of influencers under his umbrella. The company is wildly successful! It is crazy. Probably doing better than all of us."

Brandon Carter

Best-Selling Author and Celebrity Fitness Influencer from New York

"One of the things in the AI Empowerment Workshop for CEOs is how to increase productivity. AI partnered consciously does so much in the back-end to do things efficiently. Videra supports people called to make a difference in the world and use their resources to do that. We connect inspired change-makers at a Soul-level. We created a brand-identity, a voice, and now anything we produce has brand harmony in the same tone as our business. I am a mother, and it has been difficult for my business partner and I to create what we wanted, but this workshop really helped to collapse time. It has been really empowering to come together to learn these skills and give us another business partner to take our vision and mission and to integrate it."

"Because of the workshop, every day we have more time to spend with people we love, and these tools help me to spend less time on my business and focus more time on shifts I want to make and create a ripple effect starting within my own home."

Carie Bailey

Co-Founder of Videra from Florida

"The AI workshop taught me about all the tools that can make my workflow more efficient. I'm using the AI tools to help with video, image, text, and anything that requires more than an hour of work to be more efficient. I used AI for sales copy, images, website video... it is all AI."

Jose Laveaga

CEO of Vanity Data Sheet from Mexico City

"We are a company that helps digital nomads launch companies in different parts of the world. The workshop was great."

"Your workflow becomes so much easier when you integrate AI into your processes. When you use it as a process, life becomes so easier. The workshop introduced me to a lot of new tools, and I use it for different aspects of my life and become better through practices so my employees can make their life easier."

"The tools used to formulate the initial part of business helped with logos, sales copy, marketing, video creation, audios... I learned there are a lot of advancements in the AI technology space, and you need to be flexible and learn the foundational skillset so you can upscale yourself when new tools come out."

Kabir Rajput

CEO of Lewe Traveler from India

"I really gained a lot of benefit from the AI Empowerment Workshop for CEOs. Before the workshop, I had a limited understanding of AI and its uses. I can be now far more effective. I have shifted my entire business model. I am custom-creating GPTs to fit the specific needs of my business and personal life. I'm excited about having a custom tool that can benefit my industry and work. I have already implemented all the AI tools to create e-books and moved it into the creation of my daily habits. Everything has incorporated AI."

Kristin van Wey

Co-Founder of Videra from Nashville

"I learned from the AI Empowerment for CEOs, a lot of stuff, but the most important this is to optimize time, make things easier, and with much less effort so you can focus a lot less on building info products, and focus more on marketing and selling. Because of the workshop, I have more time to focus on the more important stuff. The stuff that took months to create now takes weeks, so I have more time to test new products. When I started using a lot of tools I learned at the workshop, it helped me a lot. It really is helping me and optimizing everything."

Luciano Singer

CEO of LESE Publishing from Uruguay

Nikky Kho delivers a powerful talk on AI and how to leverage to grow your business.

Lara Stein

Founder of TedX from New York

I was speaking at the main stage with Richard Branson and his mentor was a guy over in Europe that was putting on this World Speaker Summit, and the person told me I got to get you to come speak so I fly all the way over to Europe. I get there and I present and meet Nick who is doing events all over the world. He invited me to a mastermind at Tony Hsieh's and we became friends and has very interesting ideas.

Dave VanHoose

CEO at SpeakingEmpire.com from Florida

"I just wanted to extend a heartfelt thank you for the amazing AI training you provided. Your material was incredibly informative, and I genuinely enjoyed diving into it. I'm already a seasoned professional in the AI industry working mostly in the CRM space, and your training has added valuable insights to my expertise."

Clay Waugh

SR Salesforce Solutions Architect from Utah

THE IDEAL SPEAKER FOR YOUR NEXT EVENT

If your organization is looking to unlock the potential of your team and transform them into extraordinary performers, then hiring Nikky, Nikhal, and Real AI Dynamics for a keynote or workshop training is your next move!

Through cutting-edge AI-driven strategies and actionable insights, Nikky Kho has empowered businesses around the world to supercharge their teams, streamline operations, and dominate their industries. Whether you need a high-energy keynote speech to inspire or an interactive workshop to teach practical skills, Nikky will tailor the experience to meet your organization's unique needs.

5 Reasons Nikky Kho Is Booked to Speak at Events

1. **Proven AI Innovation Leader:**
   Nikky has spearheaded AI strategies for businesses worldwide, transforming how they operate and scale.

2. **Tailored Insights for CEOs:**
   His experience in guiding executive teams ensures that his strategies are actionable and aligned with the needs of top-level leadership.

3. **Global Entrepreneurial Experience:**

Having worked across Silicon Valley, Wall Street, and international startups, Nikky brings a unique perspective that resonates with diverse business cultures.

4. **Future-Proofing Businesses:**
   Nikky's talks focus on the future of AI and how organizations can stay competitive by adopting AI-driven solutions.

5. **Concrete Steps for Growth:**
   Nikky captivates audiences by offering concrete steps that executives can implement immediately to drive growth.

Topics for CEOs from Nikky Kho's Book "Unlock AI Mastery"

Topic 1: AI-Powered Business Growth

Discover how AI can be integrated across marketing, sales, and operations to drive exponential growth and efficiency.

Topic 2: The Future of AI in Leadership

Learn how AI is reshaping executive decision-making, enabling leaders to make more informed, data-driven decisions.

Topic 3: AI Selling Systems for Revenue Acceleration

How to use AI-driven sales models to scale your business and outpace the competition.

A Personal Message for You

"In today's rapidly evolving world, artificial intelligence is no longer a concept of the future; it's the key to unlocking unprecedented growth and innovation. As the CEO of Real AI Dynamics, I've had the privilege of helping global leaders transform their businesses by leveraging cutting-edge AI strategies. I look forward to empowering you and your organization to stay ahead in this new digital landscape. Let's explore the immense opportunities AI presents and how we can embrace change together."

All the best,

Nikky Kho

5 Reasons Nikhal Ghai Is Booked to Speak at Events

1. **Youthful Innovation Expert:**
    Starting his entrepreneurial journey at just 12, Nikhal embodies the spirit of innovation and has successfully translated this into actionable AI strategies for global businesses.

2. **Operations and AI Integration Specialist:**
    His hands-on experience in operational management and integrating AI at scale ensures that his insights are both practical and transformative for executive audiences.

3. **International Entrepreneurship and Sales:**
    With a background spanning international startups and ventures, Nikhal offers a unique, globally informed perspective on leveraging technology for business success.

4. **Practical AI Applications:**
    Focused on the real-world applications of AI, Nikhal's sessions provide tangible strategies for harnessing technology to enhance operational efficiency and business growth.

5. **Engaging and Inspirational Speaker:**
    Known for his dynamic presentation style, Nikhal inspires his audiences to embrace AI with practical and visionary steps that can be implemented immediately.

Don't miss this opportunity to turn your team into a powerhouse!

Book Nikky Kho, Nikhal Ghai & Real AI Dynamics for your next event and watch your team reach new heights!

A Personal Message for You

"In a world where innovation is paramount, I've been fortunate to blend my early passion for problem-solving with the transformative power of AI. As Co-Founder and Head of Operations at Real AI Dynamics, my focus is on turning ambitious visions into reality by empowering businesses through intelligent AI solutions. I am dedicated to navigating this digital revolution alongside you, ensuring your organization not only survives but thrives. Together, we will harness the potential of AI to create a future where technology amplifies our capabilities."

All the best,

Nikhal Ghai

Unlock AI Mastery at Exclusive Pricing for Event Attendees

If your group has invited Real AI Dynamics to speak, you are entitled to an exclusive discount on the *Unlock AI Mastery* best-selling book.

Enjoy this special pricing as our way of expressing gratitude for engaging with us!

QTY.	Pricing
5-20	$21.95
21-99	$19.95
100-499	$17.95
500-999	$15.95
1000+	$13.95

To Place Your Order, Contact: support@realaidynamics.com

Table of Contents

Module 1
Introduction

As businesses navigate the rapidly evolving digital landscape, artificial intelligence (AI) is emerging as a transformative force, offering new opportunities for innovation, growth, and competitive advantage. This *AI Business* book is designed to equip you with the knowledge, skills, and strategies needed to harness the power of AI for your organization.

Get ready to embark on an immersive journey that will unlock the potential of AI and position your business for success in the future.

Introduction

The book will provide a comprehensive introduction to the world of AI in business. We'll kick off with a thought-provoking discussion on the transformative potential of AI, followed by an overview of the latest AI tools and technologies. Our exploration will continue with real-world case studies showcasing successful AI implementations across various industries.

The Potential of AI in Business

AI is rapidly reshaping the business landscape, offering unprecedented opportunities for innovation, efficiency, and growth. In this introductory session, we'll explore the transformative potential of AI across various business functions, from marketing and sales to operations and customer service. Get ready to have your mind expanded as we uncover the game-changing impact of AI.

Understanding AI Capabilities and AI Tools and Technologies

Artificial Intelligence encompasses a diverse range of tools and technologies, each with its own unique capabilities and applications. In this session, we'll delve into the world of machine learning, natural language processing, computer vision, and more. Gain a solid understanding of these cutting-edge technologies and how they can be leveraged to drive business success.

Real-World AI Applications

AI is no longer a futuristic concept; it's already transforming businesses across various sectors. From healthcare and finance to manufacturing and retail, we'll explore real-world examples of AI applications that are revolutionizing industries. Discover how companies are leveraging AI to streamline operations, enhance customer experiences, and gain a competitive edge.

Implementing AI in Business Processes

AI in Marketing

Discover how AI can revolutionize your marketing efforts by enhancing personalization, optimizing campaigns, and delivering data-driven insights. Explore applications such as chatbots, predictive analytics, and content generation, empowering you to connect with your audience more effectively and drive better results.

AI in Sales

Transform your sales processes with the power of AI. Learn how to leverage AI-driven predictive models, intelligent lead scoring, and conversational AI assistants to streamline your sales cycle, improve lead management, and close deals more efficiently.

AI in Human Resources

Discover how AI can revolutionize your HR practices, from streamlining recruitment and onboarding processes to enhancing employee engagement and development. Learn about AI-powered tools for résumé screening, talent acquisition, and workforce analytics, empowering you to attract and retain top talent.

AI in Finance

Explore the potential of AI in finance, from automating financial processes and improving risk management to enabling advanced predictive analytics and fraud detection. Gain insights into how AI can enhance decision-making, optimize resource allocation, and drive financial performance.

Avoiding Common Pitfalls

Lack of Clear Strategy

Failing to develop a well-defined AI strategy aligned with your business objectives can lead to misaligned initiatives, wasted resources, and suboptimal results. Ensure your AI efforts are guided by a clear roadmap and measurable goals.

Data Quality Issues

AI systems are only as good as the data they are trained on. Inaccurate, incomplete, or biased data can significantly impact the performance and reliability of your AI solutions. Implement robust data governance practices to ensure data integrity and quality.

Security and Privacy Concerns

As AI becomes more prevalent, it is crucial to address potential security and privacy risks. Develop robust policies and protocols to protect sensitive data, ensure compliance with regulations, and maintain the trust of your customers and stakeholders.

Skill Gaps and Change Management

Integrating AI into your business may require upskilling your workforce and addressing potential resistance to change. Invest in training programs and change management strategies to ensure a smooth transition and maximize the benefits of AI adoption.

Tool Integration Process

1. Select AI Tool
   Identify the most suitable AI tool based on the specific business requirements and objectives.
2. **Configure and Train**
   Customize the AI tool's parameters and train it using relevant data to align with the desired outcomes.
3. **Integrate and Deploy**

Seamlessly integrate the AI tool into the existing business process, ensuring smooth operation and user adoption.

4. **Monitor and Optimize**
   Continuously monitor the AI tool's performance, gather feedback, and make necessary adjustments for optimal results.

Developing an AI-Driven Strategy

As businesses embrace the transformative power of AI, developing a comprehensive and well-executed AI strategy becomes paramount. In this section, we'll explore a robust framework for creating an AI-driven strategy that aligns with your organization's goals and positions you for long-term success.

Creating a Strategic AI Roadmap

Establish a clear roadmap for your AI journey by defining your vision, objectives, and key performance indicators. This strategic roadmap will serve as a guiding light, ensuring that your AI initiatives are focused, measurable, and aligned with your overall business strategy.

Aligning AI Initiatives with Business Goals

Successful AI adoption requires a seamless integration of AI initiatives with your core business objectives.

In this book, we'll explore frameworks and methodologies for identifying and prioritizing AI use cases that directly contribute to your organization's goals, whether it's enhancing customer experiences, optimizing operations, or driving revenue growth.

The book will cover various AI topics, from the fundamentals to cutting-edge technologies and real-world applications.

Experts from leading tech companies will share their experiences, challenges, and best practices in AI development and deployment.

Introduction to Artificial Intelligence

Discover the revolutionary field of artificial intelligence (AI) and how it is transforming industries worldwide. Explore the core concepts, technologies, and applications that are driving this exciting new era of innovation.

What is AI and How It's Transforming Industries?

Artificial Intelligence (AI) is the field of computer science that enables machines to perform human-like tasks, such as learning, problem-solving, and decision-making.

AI is revolutionizing various industries, from healthcare to transportation, by automating repetitive tasks, enhancing customer experiences, and driving innovation.

The Rise of AI and Its Future Impact

Artificial intelligence has seen rapid advancements in recent years, driven by the availability of big data, increased computing power, and innovative algorithms. As AI continues to evolve, it is poised to transform industries, reshape the workforce, and impact our daily lives in profound ways. From automating mundane tasks to powering autonomous vehicles, AI is revolutionizing how we live and work. Experts predict AI will create new job opportunities, enhance productivity, and unlock groundbreaking innovations across sectors like healthcare, finance, and transportation.

Key AI Technologies and Applications

Machine Learning: Algorithms that enable computers to learn and improve from experience, powering predictive models and decision-making.

Natural Language Processing (NLP): Techniques that allow computers to analyze, understand, and generate human language, enabling chatbots and language translation.

Computer Vision: Technologies that enable computers to identify and process images and videos, used in facial recognition, self-driving cars, and medical imaging.

Supervised, Unsupervised, and Reinforcement Learning
Unsupervised Learning

1. Supervised Learning:

Algorithms trained on labeled data to predict outputs for new inputs. Useful for classification and regression tasks.

2. Unsupervised Learning:

Algorithms that discover patterns in unlabeled data. Helps identify hidden structures and groupings without predefined targets.

3. Reinforcement Learning:

Agents learn by interacting with an environment, receiving rewards or penalties to optimize their behavior. Suitable for decision-making and controlling problems.

4. Neural Networks and Deep Learning

Neural networks are a powerful machine learning technique inspired by the human brain. Deep learning, a subset of neural networks, has revolutionized fields like computer vision and natural language processing. These AI models learn complex patterns in data by passing it through multiple layers of artificial neurons, enabling them to tackle problems that traditional algorithms struggle with.

5. Natural Language Processing and Computer Vision
Natural Language Processing (NLP):

NLP is the field of AI that enables machines to understand, interpret, and generate human language. It powers chatbots, language translation, sentiment analysis, and more.

Computer Vision:

This is the field of AI that enables machines to interpret and understand digital images and videos. It facilitates facial recognition, object detection, image classification, and other visual AI applications.

AI Ethics and Responsible AI

1. **Ensuring Fairness and Non-discrimination**
   Developing AI systems that are unbiased and treat all individuals equitably, regardless of race, gender, or other personal attributes.

2. **Preserving Privacy and Data Rights**
   Protecting the privacy of individuals whose data is used to train AI models and giving them control over how their information is used.

3. **Promoting Transparency and Explainability**
   Designing AI systems that can explain their decision-making processes, so users understand how conclusions are reached.

4. **Mitigating Negative Societal Impacts**
   Anticipating and addressing the potential harms that AI could pose to communities, the workforce, and society at large.

The AI Talent Landscape and In-Demand Skills

Cognitive Skills: Strong problem-solving, critical thinking, and analytical abilities are essential for success in the AI field.

Programming Expertise: Proficiency in programming languages like Python, R, and JavaScript is highly valued for AI development.

Data Fluency: The ability to work with large datasets, clean and process data, and extract insights is crucial.

Machine Learning: Strong understanding of machine learning algorithms, neural networks, and deep learning techniques is in high demand.

Accessing AI Tools and Resources: AI Tools and Platforms. Explore a wide range of open-source and commercial AI tools, from machine learning frameworks to natural language processing APIs, to accelerate your AI development.

AI Datasets: Leverage curated datasets spanning computer vision, natural language, speech, and more to train and test your AI models effectively.

AI Education Resources: Access a wealth of online courses, tutorials, and documentation to deepen your understanding of AI concepts, algorithms, and best practices.

AI Community: Connect with a vibrant global community of AI enthusiasts, researchers, and practitioners to share knowledge, collaborate, and stay up to date on the latest advancements. *(If you are reading this book, you will be provided access to our community.)*

As we welcome you again to our AI book! We're thrilled to have you join us on this exciting journey to explore the transformative power of artificial intelligence. Let's start by setting the tone for an engaging, enriching, and collaborative learning experience for you to read.

Defining the Book's Scope and Focus

Comprehensive AI Introduction: The book will provide a comprehensive overview of artificial intelligence, covering key concepts, technologies, and real-world applications.

Hands-On Skill Development: Readers will engage in practical exercises and projects to gain hands-on experience with AI tools and techniques.

Industry Relevance: The curriculum will be tailored to address the most in-demand AI skills and applications across various industries.

Module 2

WHAT IS "AI"?

Artificial Intelligence (AI)

Artificial Intelligence (AI) is a dynamic and rapidly evolving field of computer science that focuses on developing intelligent machines capable of performing tasks traditionally requiring human intelligence. These tasks include learning, problem-solving, decision-making, perception, and even understanding natural language.

AI systems have become increasingly sophisticated, leveraging advanced algorithms and computational power to analyze vast amounts of data, uncover complex patterns, and derive insights that enhance human capabilities. Whether through machine learning, neural networks, or natural language processing, AI's ability to automate complex processes has transformed industries, enabling businesses to:

- Optimize operations.
- Predict market trends.
- Provide personalized customer experiences.

As AI technology continues to evolve, it is increasingly integrated into daily life, from virtual assistants and recommendation systems to healthcare diagnostics and autonomous vehicles.

The foundation of AI lies in its capacity to mimic certain aspects of human thought processes. This involves not only analyzing data but also learning from it to improve over time.

Key areas include:

- **Machine Learning**: A subset of AI that allows systems to adapt and improve performance without explicit programming for every scenario.
- **Deep Learning**: Utilizes neural networks modeled after the human brain to recognize patterns in large datasets, driving advancements in image and speech recognition.

The goal of AI is not merely to replicate human intelligence but to enhance it, enabling new possibilities in fields like:

- Robotics
- Finance
- Medicine

The Rapid Advancement of AI Technology

1950s-1970s

- AI research begins with early successes in areas like game-playing and simple problem-solving, laying the foundations for future progress.

1980s-1990s

- The rise of expert systems and neural networks drives advancements in AI capabilities, leading to breakthroughs in language processing and computer vision.

2000s-2010s

- The availability of big data and increased computing power fuels a revolution in deep learning, enabling AI to excel at complex tasks like image recognition and natural language processing.

AI Tools and Platforms

- Chatbots, virtual assistants, and natural language processing tools that enable intelligent human-machine interactions.

AI Analytics

- Predictive analytics, machine learning algorithms, and data visualization tools that uncover insights from complex data.

Computer Vision

- Image and video analysis capabilities that can identify objects, detect anomalies, and automate visual tasks.

Robotic Process Automation (RPA)

- Software bots that automate repetitive, rules-based business processes to increase efficiency and reduce errors.

AI in Healthcare

AI is revolutionizing the healthcare industry, enabling advancements in disease diagnosis, personalized treatment plans, and predictive analytics. From automated imaging analysis to robotic surgery, AI-powered solutions are improving patient outcomes and streamlining clinical workflows. AI algorithms can rapidly process large datasets, identify patterns, and provide valuable insights to healthcare professionals, leading to more accurate diagnoses and more effective therapies.

AI in Finance and Banking

AI is transforming the finance and banking industry, enabling intelligent automation, fraud detection, personalized wealth management, and predictive analytics. By leveraging machine learning and natural language processing, banks can enhance customer experiences, optimize operations, and manage risk more effectively. From robot-advisors to AI-powered lending decisions, the adoption of AI technologies is enabling financial institutions to gain competitive advantages, improve decision-making, and stay ahead of evolving customer demands and regulatory requirements.

AI in Retail and E-commerce

AI is revolutionizing the retail and e-commerce industries, enabling personalized product recommendations, predictive analytics for inventory management, and seamless checkout experiences. Leveraging AI, retailers can optimize operations, enhance customer engagement, and stay ahead of the competition. From intelligent chatbots to computer vision-powered visual search, AI is empowering retailers to deliver a more convenient and tailored shopping journey for their customers, both in-store and online.

AI in Manufacturing

Artificial Intelligence is transforming the manufacturing industry, enabling greater automation, optimized production processes, and predictive maintenance. AI-powered smart factories leverage computer vision, natural language processing, and machine learning to streamline operations and boost efficiency. From predictive analytics to collaborative robotics, AI drives manufacturing innovation across sectors, from automotive to aerospace. By integrating AI, manufacturers can reduce downtime, enhance quality control, and make data-driven decisions to stay competitive.

AI in Transportation and Logistics

AI is transforming transportation and logistics by enabling autonomous vehicles, optimized routing, predictive maintenance, and intelligent supply chain management. These advancements improve efficiency, reduce costs, and enhance safety across the industry. Self-driving cars and trucks use AI-powered computer vision and decision-making to navigate roads without human intervention. AI also powers predictive analytics for fleet maintenance, optimizing vehicle usage, and preventing breakdowns.

AI in Education

AI is transforming the education sector, enabling personalized learning, intelligent tutoring systems, and automated grading. AI-powered adaptive learning platforms analyze student data to deliver customized content and support, improving outcomes and engagement. AI also assists teachers with administrative tasks, allowing them to focus more on instruction and student support. From virtual teaching assistants to AI-driven campus management, the potential of AI in education is immense.

AI in Agriculture

AI is revolutionizing the agricultural industry, driving precision farming, automated crop monitoring, and predictive analytics to optimize yields and sustainability. Advanced computer vision and machine learning enables real-time detection of pests, diseases, and nutritional deficiencies in crops. AI-powered drones and robots assist with planting, harvesting, and targeted pesticide application, reducing labor costs and environmental impact. Predictive algorithms also help farmers plan and adapt to changing weather patterns and climate conditions.

AI in Energy and Utilities

AI is revolutionizing the energy and utilities sector, enabling more efficient and sustainable power generation, distribution, and consumption. From predictive maintenance in power plants to optimizing energy grids, AI is unlocking new possibilities for the future of energy. AI-powered smart meters, predictive analytics, and automated decision-making are helping utilities better manage supply and demand, reduce waste, and provide personalized services to customers.

AI in Media and Entertainment

AI is transforming the media and entertainment industry, powering intelligent content creation, personalized recommendations, and immersive experiences. From predictive analytics to generate personalized content to AI-driven visual effects, AI is revolutionizing how audiences engage with media. Innovative AI tools are enabling content creators to streamline production workflows, enhance creativity, and deliver more engaging experiences to viewers across film, television, music, and gaming.

AI in Government and Public Sector

AI is revolutionizing the way governments and public sector organizations operate. From improving citizen services to enhancing national security, AI-powered solutions are driving efficiency, transparency, and data-driven decision-making in the public realm. AI is being leveraged in areas like predictive analytics for resource allocation, intelligent chatbots for citizen engagement, and automated document processing to streamline bureaucratic workflows.

AI in Cybersecurity

AI-powered cybersecurity tools are revolutionizing the way organizations detect, prevent, and respond to cyber threats. From advanced threat detection to autonomous incident response, AI is enhancing the security posture of businesses across industries. By leveraging machine learning and natural language processing, AI-based cybersecurity solutions can rapidly analyze vast amounts of data, identify anomalies, and take immediate action to mitigate risks, providing an unparalleled level of protection.

Ethical Considerations in AI

As AI systems become more advanced and pervasive, it is crucial to address the ethical implications of their development and deployment. Key concerns include algorithmic bias, privacy, transparency, accountability, and the impact on jobs and society. Responsible AI practices must ensure AI systems are designed and used in an ethical manner, respecting human rights, and promoting the greater good. Ongoing governance, oversight, and public dialogue are essential to guide the ethical evolution of AI technology.

Challenges and Limitations of AI Interpretability and Explainability

AI models can be complex and difficult to understand, making it challenging.to explain their decision-making processes

Bias and Fairness

AI systems can perpetuate or amplify societal biases present in the data used to train them, leading to unfair and discriminatory outcomes.

Data Dependency

AI's performance is heavily dependent on the quality and quantity of data used for training, which can be difficult to obtain or may not be representative of the real world.

Case Study: AI-Powered Predictive Maintenance in Manufacturing

In a leading manufacturing plant, AI-powered predictive maintenance is transforming operations. By analyzing real-time sensor data, the AI system predicts when equipment is likely to fail, enabling proactive maintenance schedules. This has reduced unplanned downtime by 35% and extended the lifespan of critical machinery by 18%. The AI model continuously learns from maintenance logs and sensor data to refine its predictions, driving continuous process improvements.

Case Study: AI-Driven Personalized Recommendations in Retail

AI-powered personalized recommendations have transformed the retail industry, providing customers with tailored product suggestions based on their browsing and purchase history. By leveraging machine learning algorithms, retailers can offer a highly personalized shopping experience, leading to increased customer satisfaction, loyalty, and sales.

Case Study: AI-Enabled Early Disease Detection in Healthcare

AI algorithms are revolutionizing disease diagnosis by analyzing vast troves of medical data. AI can detect subtle patterns and anomalies through machine learning, enabling early identification of conditions like cancer, Alzheimer's, and heart disease before symptoms appear. This empowers doctors to intervene sooner, leading to better outcomes and reduced healthcare costs. AI-powered screening is proving invaluable, especially in underserved communities with limited specialist access.

Case Study: AI-Powered Autonomous Vehicles in Transportation

Autonomous vehicles powered by AI are revolutionizing the transportation industry. These self-driving cars use advanced sensors, machine learning algorithms, and neural networks to perceive their surroundings, make real-time decisions, and navigate roads safely without human intervention. By automating the driving process, autonomous vehicles have the potential to reduce accidents, ease traffic congestion, and provide mobility for those who cannot drive. Pilot programs and real-world deployments are already showcasing the transformative impact of this technology.

Case Study: AI-Driven Fraud Detection in Banking

Banks are increasingly leveraging AI technology to combat the growing threat of financial fraud. AI-powered fraud detection systems analyze massive amounts of transaction data in real time, identifying suspicious patterns and anomalies that would be impossible for humans to detect. By applying machine learning algorithms, these systems can automatically flag potentially fraudulent activities, allowing banks to take swift action and protect their customers' accounts. This has proven highly effective in reducing fraud losses and enhancing the overall security of banking operations.

Case Study: AI-Enabled Personalized Learning in Education

Imagine a classroom where each student receives a tailored learning experience powered by AI. This revolutionary approach adapts lesson plans, content, and pace to individual needs, ensuring no learner gets left behind. By leveraging data analytics and machine learning, AI-driven personalized learning platforms identify knowledge gaps, recommend supplementary materials, and provide real-time feedback to teachers, empowering them to better support their students.

Future Trends and Advancements in AI

Continued Exponential Growth: AI technology is evolving at a rapid pace, with computational power, data availability, and algorithm sophistication increasing exponentially.

Expanded Real-World Applications: AI will be integrated into an even wider range of industries and applications, from healthcare and transportation to education and sustainability.

Increased Autonomy and Intelligence: AI systems will become more autonomous, with the ability to learn, reason, and make decisions with less human intervention.

Conclusion: Unlocking the Full Potential of AI

As we've explored, artificial intelligence holds immense potential to transform industries, drive innovation, and improve lives. By embracing AI technologies and overcoming ethical challenges, we can unlock unprecedented possibilities and usher in a new era of progress and prosperity.

Module 3

Introduction to AI Tools for Business Solutions

Module 3 provides a comprehensive overview of how artificial intelligence is transforming the business landscape, unlocking unprecedented opportunities for growth, efficiency, and innovation.

In today's digital age, AI-powered tools offer businesses a competitive edge by:

- Automating complex tasks
- Enhancing customer experience
- Providing deep, data-driven insights that were once unimaginable

These tools are no longer reserved for tech giants; they are accessible to businesses of all sizes, enabling companies to optimize their operations and make informed, real-time decisions.

Key Advantages of AI-Powered Tools

Streamlining Workflows:

AI-powered tools can automate repetitive tasks, such as:

- Data entry
- Scheduling
- Customer inquiries

This automation frees up valuable human resources, allowing employees to focus on more strategic and creative initiatives. For example:

- **AI-driven chatbots** handle customer service inquiries 24/7, providing instant responses and personalized interactions that improve the overall customer experience.
- **Predictive analytics** allows businesses to forecast trends, customer behaviors, and operational needs with remarkable accuracy, enabling companies to anticipate market changes and adjust their strategies accordingly to stay ahead of the competition.

Unlocking Valuable Insights:

AI tools analyze large data sets to:

- Identify patterns and trends
- Develop personalized marketing strategies
- Improve product development
- Optimize supply chains

This data-driven approach enhances decision-making and helps businesses identify new revenue streams and areas for growth.

Scalability:

AI tools can grow with your business. As your company expands, these technologies:

- Continue to support your evolving needs
- Provide consistent and reliable performance

Transforming Business Solutions

The integration of AI into business solutions doesn't just improve efficiency—it transforms how businesses operate, innovate, and engage with their customers.

The adoption of AI tools has become essential for organizations looking to remain competitive in an increasingly data-driven world.

As we move into the next section of this module, we'll explore the rich history of AI, tracing its development from early computational theories to the sophisticated systems of today. This historical context will provide valuable insights into how AI has evolved into the transformative force driving modern business solutions.

Importance of Selecting the Right AI Tools

Selecting the right AI tools is critical to the success of any business looking to leverage artificial intelligence for growth and efficiency. AI has the power to transform business processes, offering advanced solutions that can:

- Automate repetitive tasks
- Enhance decision-making
- Provide valuable insights into customer behavior and operational efficiency

However, not every AI tool is suitable for every business need. Choosing the wrong tool can lead to:

- Inefficiencies

- Wasted resources
- Missed opportunities

The right AI solution should align closely with specific business goals to ensure that investments in technology contribute directly to outcomes.

Key Reasons to Select the Right AI Tool

1. Improve Operational Efficiency and Productivity:

- Streamline workflows, reducing manual tasks
- Analyze vast amounts of data quickly and accurately
- Integrate seamlessly with existing systems and processes

Choosing the wrong tool can lead to costly reconfigurations or complex adaptations, disrupting smooth operations.

2. Scalability for Growth:

- Support business expansion without overhauling systems
- Accommodate increased data, user interactions, or complex tasks
- Help businesses remain flexible and competitive

A scalable tool reduces costs for new technology or retraining employees, ensuring long-term growth and effectiveness.

3. Reliability and Accuracy:

- Provide trustworthy, data-driven insights
- Enable automated decision-making and personalized customer experiences

- Depend on robust algorithms for consistent and accurate results

Flawed tools can lead to poor analysis and decisions, harming business operations.

Unlocking Business Potential

The right AI tools can unlock unprecedented business opportunities, driving innovation and improving operational efficiency.

Competitive Advantage

Selecting the optimal AI tools can give your organization a competitive edge, allowing you to outpace rivals and dominate the market.

Enhancing Decision-Making

AI-powered tools can provide data-driven insights to support strategic decision-making, leading to more informed and impactful choices.

Streamlining Workflows

The right AI tools can automate repetitive tasks, streamline processes, and free up valuable human resources for higher-value work.

Identifying Your Business Needs and Goals

- Clearly define your business objectives and main points that you aim to solve with AI technology.

- Assess your current workflows, processes, and areas where AI could drive efficiency, productivity, or innovation.
- Prioritize your key use cases and identify the specific AI capabilities required to address them, such as natural language processing, computer vision, or predictive analytics.

Exploring Popular AI Tools and Their Capabilities:

Analytics and Insights: AI-powered analytics tools can uncover hidden patterns, trends, and actionable insights from your data to drive informed business decisions.

Conversational AI: Chatbots and virtual assistants leveraging natural language processing can automate customer service, provide product recommendations, and enhance user engagement.

Computer Vision: AI-powered computer vision solutions can automate visual inspection, object detection, and image recognition tasks to improve efficiency and accuracy.

Factors to Consider When Selecting AI Tools:

Business Alignment: Ensure the AI tools you select closely match your business objectives, workflows, and industry requirements.

Ease of Use: Choose tools that are intuitive, with a user-friendly interface, to enable seamless adoption by your team.

Scalability: Evaluate the tool's ability to scale as your business needs grow, both in terms of data volume and user base.

Integration Capability: Assess how well the AI tools can integrate with your existing enterprise systems and software stack.

Assessing Tool Integration and Scalability

Evaluate Integration Capabilities: Assess how seamlessly the AI tool integrates with your existing systems, workflows, and data sources.

Gauge Scalability Potential: Determine if the AI tool can handle increases in data volume, user demands, and business growth over time.

Analyze Deployment Complexity: Consider the technical complexity and resources required to implement and maintain the AI tool within your organization.

Ensuring Data Privacy and Security with AI Tools: Protecting sensitive data is paramount when deploying AI tools. Robust security measures, including encryption, access controls, and data governance policies, are essential to safeguard confidential information and ensure compliance with data privacy regulations.

Implementing rigorous data anonymization techniques can help minimize the risk of exposing personal or proprietary data during AI model training and deployment.

Hands-on Exercise at Home – Comparing AI Tool Features

Feature Matrix: Create a comprehensive feature matrix to compare the capabilities, limitations, and pricing of different AI tools side-by-side.

Ease of Use: Assess the user-friendliness and intuitiveness of each AI tool's interface and workflows.

Integration Capabilities: Evaluate how well the AI tools integrate with your existing business systems and processes.

Performance Benchmarking: Run test cases and measure the accuracy, speed, and scalability of each AI tool for your specific use case.

Evaluating Cost and Pricing Models of AI Tools: Selecting the right AI tools for your business requires careful consideration of the associated costs and pricing models. Understanding the various pricing structures, including subscription fees, usage-based pricing, and enterprise licensing, can help you make an informed decision that aligns with your budget and long-term needs.

Subscription Fees: Many AI tools offer a subscription-based model, where you pay a recurring monthly or annual fee to access the platform and its features. This can provide predictable costs and scalability as your usage grows.

Usage-Based Pricing: Some AI tools charge based on your actual usage, such as the number of API calls, data processing volume, or the number of users. This model can be more flexible but may be harder to budget for, especially if your needs fluctuate.

Enterprise Licensing: Larger organizations may benefit from enterprise-level licensing agreements, which can offer volume discounts, custom features, and dedicated support. This model is typically better suited for organizations with more predictable and long-term AI tool requirements.

When evaluating AI tool costs, it's also important to consider any additional fees for data storage, integration, or professional services. Understanding the total cost of ownership can help you make a more informed decision and ensure that the AI investment aligns with your overall business strategy.

Addressing AI Tool Implementation Challenges

Implementing AI tools in a business environment often comes with significant challenges, particularly around technical complexity. Integrating AI systems with existing infrastructure, such as customer relationship management (CRM) platforms, enterprise resource planning (ERP) systems, or other business-critical software, requires careful planning.

Ensuring seamless communication between AI tools and these systems can be technically demanding. This includes compatibility issues, data migration, and the need for specialized expertise to implement the integration successfully. Moreover, AI models are only as good as the data they process, so ensuring the availability of accurate, comprehensive, and clean data is essential. Poor data quality can lead to inaccurate predictions or insights, which can compromise the effectiveness of the AI tool.

Another key challenge in AI tool adoption is managing organizational change. Introducing AI technologies can face resistance from employees and stakeholders who may fear disruption or job displacement. Effective change management strategies are essential to address these concerns and gain buy-in across the organization.

This often involves clear communication about the benefits of AI, along with training programs to upskill employees. Leadership support is also critical in fostering a culture that embraces technological innovation.

By addressing both the technical and organizational aspects, businesses can overcome barriers to AI tool integration and unlock the full potential of these technologies.

Developing a Proof of Concept for AI Implementation:

Here are some key steps to ensure the solution addresses a real business need and delivers measurable value.

I. Define Use Case:

The first step is identifying a business problem that AI can solve. This requires analyzing the business's current challenges, pain points, and opportunities where automation, data analysis, or predictive capabilities could offer improvement. A well-defined use case should be narrowly focused on a tangible problem with clear outcomes, such as improving customer service with AI-powered chatbots or optimizing inventory management through predictive analytics.

II. Gather Data:

Once the use case is identified, the next step is to gather relevant data to train and test the AI model. Data is the foundation of any AI solution, and it is crucial to collect accurate, clean, and comprehensive datasets. Depending on the use case, this data can come from various sources such as databases, CRM systems, or IoT devices. Ensuring the data is well-structured and free from bias is also essential to train an AI model effectively and generate meaningful insights.

III. Build a Prototype:

After gathering the data, developing a minimum viable product (MVP) or prototype is next. This prototype serves as an initial version of the AI solution, designed to demonstrate how AI can address the use case. The goal here is not to build a full-scale product but rather to create a working model that can showcase the core functionality of the AI, proving that the concept is feasible and valuable.

IV. Test and Iterate:

The final step is to test the prototype in a real-world environment and gather feedback from key stakeholders. This phase allows you to evaluate the AI solution's performance, identify shortcomings, and refine the model based on the feedback received. Iteration is key in this stage, as the proof of concept should be continuously improved until it reliably solves the business problem and meets the desired objectives.

Incorporating User Feedback and Iterating on AI Tools: Regularly soliciting feedback from users is crucial for refining and enhancing AI tools. This helps identify pain points, uncover new use cases, and ensure the technology aligns with evolving business needs.

Iterative Improvements: By acting on user feedback, organizations can continuously optimize AI tools through software updates, feature enhancements, and UI/UX refinements. This agile approach keeps the technology relevant and impactful.

Collaborative Iteration: Engaging cross-functional stakeholders, from IT to business units, ensures a holistic view of AI tool performance and facilitates a collaborative approach to ongoing improvements.

Designing AI-Powered Business Solutions: Brainstorm innovative ways to leverage AI in your business. Identify pain points and opportunities where AI can drive efficiency, enhance customer experience, or unlock new revenue streams.

Prototyping: Develop a proof of concept to test your AI-powered solution. Validate your assumptions, gather user feedback, and refine your approach before full-scale implementation.

Collaboration: Bring together cross-functional teams to design the AI solution. Leverage diverse perspectives and expertise to create a holistic, user-centric experience.

Data-Driven Design: Analyze relevant data to inform your AI-powered solution. Ensure your design is grounded in real-world insights and customer needs.

Leveraging AI Tools for Process Automation

AI tools can revolutionize your business operations by automating repetitive, time-consuming tasks. From data entry to customer service, AI-powered automation can streamline your workflows, boost efficiency, and free up your employees to focus on higher-value activities.

By integrating AI-driven automation into your existing systems and processes, you can improve accuracy, consistency, and speed across your organization. This can lead to cost savings, increased productivity, and enhanced customer satisfaction.

Brainstorming AI Use Cases

Enhancing Customer Experience with AI Tools: AI-powered chatbots and virtual assistants can provide personalized, 24/7 support to your customers, addressing their queries and concerns efficiently. AI-driven recommendations and predictive analytics can also help anticipate customer needs and offer tailored products or services, boosting customer satisfaction and loyalty.

Evaluating AI Tool Governance:

Accountability: Ensure clear lines of responsibility for AI tool performance and decisions. Establish processes for monitoring and addressing issues.

Transparency: Promote transparency around AI model development, data usage, and decision-making. Provide visibility into the "black box" of AI systems.

Ethical Principles: Align AI tool governance with core ethical principles like fairness, privacy, and explainability. Establish a framework for ethical AI deployment.

Driving Innovation and Competitive Advantage with AI:

AI Tools Automate Repetitive Tasks: Optimize workflows and unlock new efficiencies, driving innovation across your organization.

Gain Competitive Edge: Leverage AI to uncover valuable insights, make data-driven decisions, and deliver superior products or services that set you apart in the market.

Accelerate Growth: AI enables businesses to scale faster, adapt to changing customer needs, and seize new opportunities for expansion and profitability.

Developing an AI Tool Roadmap: Analyze your existing AI tools, their capabilities, and areas for improvement

Define Business Goals: Clearly articulate the objectives you want to achieve with AI tools, aligned with your overall business strategy.

Prioritize Use Cases: Identify the most promising AI use cases that can deliver immediate value and drive long-term transformation.

Evaluate AI Tools: Research and assess the AI tools that best fit your requirements, considering factors like functionality, scalability, and integration.

Create Roadmap: Develop a comprehensive plan for AI tool implementation, with timelines, resource allocation, and milestones to track progress.

Iterate and Refine: Continuously monitor the performance of your AI tools, gather user feedback, and make adjustments to your roadmap as needed.

Ethical Considerations in AI Tool Deployment: Deploying AI tools requires careful consideration of ethical implications. Responsible AI development must prioritize fairness, transparency, and accountability to mitigate biases and protect user privacy. Organizations should establish clear guidelines for ethical AI use, including mechanisms for monitoring model performance and addressing algorithmic biases.

Presenting AI-powered solutions: Craft a Compelling Narrative:

Tell a story that showcases how your AI-powered solution addresses your client's key challenges and objectives. Weave in real-world examples and data to build credibility.

Highlight Key Features: Demonstrate the unique capabilities of your AI tools, focusing on the features that provide the most value to your client. Use visual aids to bring your presentation to life.

Showcase Practical Applications: Walk through a live demo or simulation to illustrate how the AI solution can be easily integrated and leveraged within your client's existing workflows and processes.

Address Concerns and Questions: Anticipate your client's questions and proactively address any concerns they may have about implementation, data privacy, or the overall impact of the AI solution.

Measuring the Impact of AI tools on Your Business: Evaluating the success of your AI tool deployment is crucial for ensuring long-term business impact. By tracking key metrics, you can optimize your AI strategy and demonstrate the value of your investments.

- **Process Efficiency:** Measure improvements in operational efficiency, such as reduced manual effort or faster decision-making, enabled by AI automation.

- **Cost Savings:** Quantify the financial benefits of AI, including reduced labor costs, improved resource utilization, and enhanced productivity.
- **Customer Satisfaction:** Track improvements in customer experience, such as faster response times, more personalized recommendations, and higher retention rates.

Revenue Growth:

Assess the impact of AI-powered insights and predictions on revenue generation, such as increased sales, upsells, and cross-sells. By regularly monitoring these key performance indicators, you can demonstrate the value of your AI investments and continuously refine your approach to drive greater business impact.

Key Insights for AI Tool Implementation

Start with a Strategic Vision:

Before diving into AI tool implementation, it's crucial to have a clear strategic vision that aligns with your organization's overall objectives. Understanding how AI can support your business goals helps in choosing the right tools and approaches. This vision should guide your AI initiatives, ensuring they contribute to long-term value rather than being isolated experiments.

Build on Solid Data Foundations:

AI's effectiveness is deeply rooted in the quality and availability of data. Ensure you have robust data governance, quality control processes, and infrastructure in place. A common insight from successful AI implementations is that the time and resources invested in preparing, cleaning, and organizing data significantly enhance the outcomes of AI projects.

Focus on User Adoption and Change Management:

The success of AI tools doesn't just depend on their technical capabilities but also on how well they are adopted by the users within the organization. Effective change management practices are essential. This includes training, user support, and clear communication about the benefits and changes brought by AI tools. Engaging users early and addressing their feedback helps in tailoring AI solutions to meet real needs and ensures smoother integration into daily operations.

Ensure Ethical and Responsible Use of AI

As AI becomes more integrated into business processes, ethical considerations and responsible use of AI are increasingly important. This includes ensuring data privacy, avoiding bias in AI models, and being transparent about how AI decisions are made. Establishing ethical guidelines and principles for AI use can help maintain trust and compliance with regulations.

Iterate and Scale with Caution

Successful AI implementation is rarely a "big bang" moment but rather a series of iterations and learning cycles. Start with pilot projects to test and learn from the deployment of AI tools in specific contexts. This approach allows for adjustments and refinements based on real-world feedback. Scaling AI solutions across the organization should be done cautiously, ensuring that the infrastructure, processes, and team capabilities are in place to support larger-scale deployments.

Tool Selection

Define Clear Objectives: Identify what you want to achieve with AI. Understanding your goals will help you select tools that are aligned with your objectives.

Assess Data Availability: Evaluate the data you have as different AI tools are optimized for different types and volumes of data. Ensure the tool you choose can handle your data efficiently.

Consider Compatibility: The AI tool should integrate seamlessly with your existing systems and infrastructure. Compatibility reduces implementation time and costs.

Evaluate Ease of Use: Look for tools that are user-friendly and require minimal training, especially if your team does not have advanced AI expertise.

Check Scalability: Choose tools that can scale with your needs. As your business grows, your AI solutions should be able to accommodate increased workloads.

Analyze Performance: Research and compare the performance of different tools for tasks similar to yours. Performance metrics can include accuracy, speed, and resource efficiency.

Review Cost: Evaluate the cost of implementation, including any subscriptions, licenses, and additional resources needed. Consider the total cost of ownership over time.

Prioritize Security: Ensure the tool meets your security requirements. This is critical for protecting sensitive data and maintaining compliance with regulations.

Seek Flexibility: Look for tools that offer customization options to tailor the AI solutions to your specific needs.

Consider the Vendor's Reputation: Choose tools from reputable vendors with a track record of success and reliability. Customer reviews and case studies can provide valuable insights.

Look for Community and Support: Tools with a strong user community and robust support services can help resolve issues quickly and offer a wealth of shared knowledge.

Check for Updates and Development: Ensure the tool is regularly updated and improved. Continuous development reflects the vendor's commitment to staying current with AI advancements.

Evaluate Ethical Considerations: Understand how the AI tool addresses ethical concerns, such as bias and transparency. Ethical AI use is increasingly important for public trust and compliance.

Assess Integration Capabilities: The ability to integrate with other tools and systems is crucial for a cohesive technology ecosystem. This includes APIs, plugins, and compatibility with other software.

Trial and Experimentation: Whenever possible, conduct a pilot project or trial to test the AI tool in your environment. Real-world testing provides insights into how well the tool meets your needs.

Pitfalls Underestimating the Importance of Data Quality and Preparation:

One of the most significant pitfalls is neglecting the quality and readiness of the data required for AI tools to function effectively. AI models and tools rely heavily on data to learn, make predictions, and generate insights. However, if the data is incomplete, biased, or poorly organized, it can lead to inaccurate outcomes, model failures, or biased decisions. Preparing data involves cleaning, structuring, and ensuring it is representative of the real-world scenarios the AI is expected to handle. Overlooking the necessity for rigorous data preparation can undermine the effectiveness of AI tools, no matter how advanced they are.

Overestimating AI Capabilities and Underestimating Human Involvement:

Another common pitfall is having unrealistic expectations about what AI tools can achieve without significant human oversight and input. There's often a misconception that AI solutions can operate autonomously right from implementation. In reality, AI systems require continuous monitoring, maintenance, and fine-tuning to perform optimally. Human expertise is crucial for interpreting AI-generated insights accurately, integrating them into decision-making processes, and ensuring they align with ethical standards. Failure to recognize the need for ongoing human involvement can lead to reliance on AI decisions that may not be appropriate or effective in all contexts, potentially leading to strategic missteps and operational inefficiencies.

Conclusion and Next Steps

We've explored the key considerations for selecting and implementing the right AI solutions to drive business success. As you move forward, it's important to develop a comprehensive AI tool roadmap and continuously measure the impact on your organization.

Module 4
Introduction to AI in Business Processes

Introduction to AI in Business Processes

Artificial Intelligence (AI) has transformed the landscape of modern business, offering unprecedented opportunities to streamline operations, enhance decision-making, and drive innovation. As organizations seek to stay competitive in an increasingly digital world, integrating AI into core business processes has become a strategic imperative. This introduction will provide a comprehensive overview of how AI can be leveraged to revolutionize the way organizations operate, highlighting key areas of application, potential benefits, and best practices for successful implementation.

The Business Case for AI Integration

Increased Operational Efficiency:

By automating repetitive tasks and optimizing workflows, AI can significantly improve productivity and reduce operational costs across an organization. AI-powered automation can handle mundane, time-consuming activities, allowing employees to focus on more strategic, value-added work. This not only streamlines business processes but also frees up resources that can be reallocated to drive innovation and growth.

Enhanced Decision-Making:

AI systems can analyze vast amounts of data, identify patterns and insights, and provide data-driven recommendations to support better, more informed decision-making. This can lead to more effective risk management, more strategic planning, and improved business outcomes. By augmenting human intelligence with AI-powered analytics, organizations can make more accurate, timely, and objective decisions, giving them a competitive edge in the market.

Improved Customer Experience:

AI-powered technologies, such as chatbots, personalized recommendations, and predictive analytics, can significantly enhance the customer experience. By anticipating customer needs, providing personalized solutions, and automating routine inquiries, organizations can build stronger, more loyal relationships with their customers. This can lead to increased customer satisfaction, reduced churn, and higher revenue growth.

Competitive Advantage:

Organizations that successfully integrate AI into their business processes can gain a significant competitive advantage in the market. By leveraging AI to streamline operations, improve decision-making, and enhance the customer experience, companies can differentiate themselves from their competitors, adapt more quickly to changing market conditions, and position themselves as industry leaders. Early adoption of AI can help organizations stay ahead of the curve and solidify their position in the marketplace.

Identify Key Business Areas for AI Implementation

Identifying the right business areas to focus AI implementation efforts is a crucial first step in any successful AI integration journey. Organizations should carefully assess their core operations, target markets, and strategic priorities to pinpoint the areas that hold the greatest potential for AI-driven improvements and innovations.

Some key business areas ripe for AI integration include:

- **Customer Service and Support:**
  AI-powered chatbots, virtual assistants, and predictive analytics can enhance the customer experience, improve response times, and reduce operational costs.
- **Sales and Marketing:**
  AI can help with lead generation, personalized product recommendations, targeted marketing campaigns, and optimizing sales funnels.
- **Supply Chain and Logistics:**
  AI-enabled demand forecasting, inventory management, route optimization, and predictive maintenance can drive greater operational efficiency.
- **Financial Operations:**
  AI can automate mundane tasks, detect fraud, provide personalized financial advice, and improve risk management and compliance.
- **Human Resources:**

AI can streamline recruiting, employee onboarding, performance management, and learning and development through intelligent automation and data-driven insights.

- **Research and Development:**
  AI-powered experimentation, prototyping, and predictive modeling can accelerate the innovation lifecycle and improve product development.

When evaluating potential use cases, organizations should consider the following factors:

- Data availability
- Business impact
- Technical feasibility
- Alignment with strategic objectives

By focusing on high-impact, low-complexity projects first, companies can:

- Build momentum
- Demonstrate early wins
- Pave the way for broader AI adoption across the enterprise.

Assessing Current Processes and Data Readiness

Evaluate Existing Business Processes:

The first step in assessing your organization's readiness for AI integration is to thoroughly evaluate your current business processes. Identify the key workflows, decision points, and pain points within your operations. Understand how information and data currently flow through your organization and where bottlenecks or inefficiencies may exist. This assessment will help you pinpoint the areas that could benefit most from AI-powered automation, optimization, and insights.

Audit Data Availability and Quality:

AI systems rely heavily on high-quality, structured data to learn and make accurate predictions. Conduct a comprehensive audit of the data you currently collect and store across your organization. Determine the completeness, accuracy, and format of this data. Identify any gaps, inconsistencies, or siloed data sources that could hinder your ability to effectively train and deploy AI models. Addressing data quality and accessibility issues will be a critical prerequisite for successful AI integration.

Assess Technical Infrastructure Readiness

Evaluate the technological capabilities of your organization to support AI-powered solutions. This includes reviewing your computing power, data storage, and networking infrastructure. Determine whether you have the necessary hardware, software, and IT expertise to handle the increased computational requirements and data management needs of AI systems. Identify any upgrades or investments that may be required to ensure your technical foundation is prepared for AI integration.

Selecting the Right AI Technologies and Solutions

Understanding AI Technologies:

Identifying the right AI technologies and solutions is a critical step in successfully implementing AI within your business processes. This requires a deep understanding of the various AI techniques, their capabilities, and how they can be applied to address your specific business needs. From machine learning algorithms to natural language processing, computer vision, and predictive analytics, the AI landscape is vast and constantly evolving.

Key Considerations for Evaluation:

When evaluating AI solutions, it's important to assess factors such as:

- Data requirements,
- Model training and deployment,
- Integration with existing systems,
- The level of human-AI collaboration required.

Additionally, considerations around scalability, explainability, and responsible AI practices should be taken into account to ensure the chosen solutions align with your organization's strategic objectives and ethical principles.

Engaging Stakeholders:

Engaging with AI vendors, industry experts, and conducting thorough proofs-of-concept can help you identify the most suitable AI technologies and develop a comprehensive roadmap for successful implementation. By aligning AI capabilities with your business priorities, you can unlock transformative opportunities to enhance process efficiency, uncover valuable insights, and drive competitive advantage.

Establishing an AI Governance Framework:

Implementing a robust AI governance framework is essential to ensure the responsible and effective deployment of AI technologies within an organization. This framework should establish clear policies, processes, and oversight mechanisms to manage the complexities and risks associated with AI systems.

Key elements of an effective AI governance framework include:

- Defining AI ethics principles.
- Establishing decision-making protocols.
- Assigning roles and responsibilities.
- Implementing data management and security controls.
- Creating transparency and accountability measures.

Organizations should also consider establishing an AI ethics board or committee to provide guidance and oversight on critical AI-related decisions. By proactively addressing governance, organizations can build trust in their AI initiatives, mitigate legal and reputational risks, and align their AI deployments with broader business objectives and societal values.

A well-designed governance framework can help organizations harness the power of AI while ensuring it is used responsibly and ethically.

Developing an AI Implementation Roadmap:

Begin by carefully evaluating your organization's existing technology infrastructure, data maturity, and digital capabilities. Identify any gaps or areas that need improvement to support the successful integration of AI. This assessment will help you develop a comprehensive roadmap that addresses your specific needs and constraints.

Prioritize Use Cases:

Collaborate with key stakeholders to identify the most promising AI use cases that align with your business objectives. Prioritize areas where AI can deliver the greatest impact, such as:

- Improving operational efficiency.
- Enhancing customer experiences.
- Driving innovation.

Consider both short-term quick wins and long-term transformative opportunities.

Define Implementation Phases:

Break down your AI implementation into manageable phases, each with clearly defined milestones and timelines. This phased approach will help you:

- Manage complexity.
- Mitigate risks.
- Ensure a smooth transition to AI-powered processes.

Assign resources, responsibilities, and success metrics for each phase to maintain accountability and track progress.

Securing Executive Sponsorship and Stakeholder Buy-In:

Engage with the C-Suite: Securing executive sponsorship is crucial for the successful implementation of AI in your business processes. Engage with the C-suite early on to align them on the strategic benefits and get their buy-in. Demonstrate how AI can:

- Drive measurable business outcomes.
- Enhance operational efficiency.
- Provide a competitive edge.

Identify Key Stakeholders:

Carefully map out all the key stakeholders who will be impacted by the integration of AI, from department heads to frontline employees. Understand their:

- Concerns.
- Pain points.
- Desired outcomes.

Proactively address their questions and involve them in the decision-making process to foster a sense of ownership and commitment.

Communicate the Vision:

Develop a clear and compelling narrative around the AI implementation journey. Use:

- Data-driven insights.

- Case studies.
- Success stories.

Illustrate the transformative potential of AI. Communicate the long-term vision and immediate benefits in a way that resonates with different stakeholder groups, ensuring they are informed, motivated, and excited about the upcoming changes.

Building Cross-Functional AI Teams:

Successful AI implementation requires a collaborative effort from diverse teams across the organization. Building cross-functional AI teams that bring together expertise from various domains, such as:

- Data science.
- IT.
- Operations.
- Marketing.
- Customer service.

These teams should work closely to:

- Identify AI opportunities.
- Develop and deploy AI models.
- Monitor their performance.

Collaboration fosters a holistic approach, ensuring that AI initiatives are aligned with business objectives and seamlessly integrated into existing workflows.

Establishing clear communication channels, shared goals, and a culture of continuous learning and innovation will enable cross-functional teams to drive AI success and delivers tangible business value.

Measuring Success and Continuous Improvement:

Implementing AI in business processes is not a one-time project but an ongoing journey. Measuring success and striving for continuous improvement is key to realizing the full potential of AI.

1. **Define clear metrics and key performance indicators (KPIs)** to evaluate the impact of AI initiatives.
2. **Regularly track and analyze these metrics** to understand the effectiveness of AI implementations and identify areas for optimization.

Foster a culture of continuous learning and improvement by encouraging:

- Experimentation.
- Feedback.
- Iteration.

By continuously refining AI models, processes, and strategies based on real-world outcomes, organizations can:

- Stay ahead of the competition.
- Drive innovation.

- Achieve sustainable growth.

Case Study: AI-Powered Predictive Maintenance in Manufacturing:

In a leading manufacturing plant, AI-powered predictive maintenance is transforming operations. By analyzing real-time sensor data, the AI system predicts when equipment is likely to fail, enabling proactive maintenance schedules. This has:

- Reduced unplanned downtime by 35%.
- Extended the lifespan of critical machinery by 18%.

The AI model continuously learns from maintenance logs and sensor data to refine its predictions, driving continuous process improvements.

Case Study: AI-Driven Personalized Recommendations in Retail

AI-powered personalized recommendations have transformed the retail industry, providing customers with tailored product suggestions based on their browsing and purchase history. By leveraging machine learning algorithms, retailers can offer a highly personalized shopping experience, leading to increased customer satisfaction, loyalty, and sales.

Case Study: AI-Enabled Early Disease Detection in Healthcare

AI algorithms are revolutionizing disease diagnosis by analyzing vast troves of medical data. AI can detect subtle patterns and anomalies through machine learning, enabling early identification of conditions like cancer, Alzheimer's, and heart disease before symptoms appear. This empowers doctors to intervene sooner, leading to better outcomes and reduced healthcare costs.

AI-powered screening is proving invaluable, especially in underserved communities with limited access to specialists.

Case Study: AI-Powered Autonomous Vehicles in Transportation

Autonomous vehicles powered by AI are revolutionizing the transportation industry. These self-driving cars use advanced sensors, machine learning algorithms, and neural networks to perceive their surroundings, make real-time decisions, and navigate roads safely without human intervention. By automating the driving process, autonomous vehicles have the potential to reduce accidents, ease traffic congestion, and provide mobility for those who cannot drive. Pilot programs and real-world deployments are already showcasing the transformative impact of this technology.

Case Study: AI-Driven Fraud Detection in Banking

Banks are increasingly leveraging AI technology to combat the growing threat of financial fraud. AI-powered fraud detection systems analyze massive amounts of transaction data in real-time, identifying suspicious patterns and anomalies that would be impossible for humans to detect. By applying machine learning algorithms, these systems can automatically flag potentially fraudulent activities, allowing banks to take swift action and protect their customers' accounts. This has proven highly effective in reducing fraud losses and enhancing the overall security of banking operations.

Case Study: AI-Enabled Personalized Learning in Education

Imagine a classroom where each student receives a tailored learning experience powered by AI. This revolutionary approach adapts lesson plans, content, and pace to individual needs, ensuring no learner gets left behind. By leveraging data analytics and machine learning, AI-driven personalized learning platforms identify knowledge gaps, recommend supplementary materials, and provide real-time feedback to teachers, empowering them to better support their students.

Future Trends and Advancements in AI

The future of AI is marked by continued exponential growth, driven by advancements in computational power, the availability of vast datasets, and increasingly sophisticated algorithms. This rapid pace of development enables AI to solve more complex problems, process larger volumes of data, and make faster, more accurate predictions.

Generative AI is advancing significantly, with models capable of creating hyper-realistic text, images, audio, and video content. These breakthroughs are already transforming industries like media, entertainment, and marketing, allowing for more creative and personalized content generation.

As AI continues to evolve, its real-world applications will expand into an even broader range of sectors. Healthcare, transportation, education, and sustainability will benefit from AI-driven innovations, leading to smarter systems and solutions for complex global challenges. AI systems are also becoming more autonomous, with the ability to learn, reason, and make decisions independently, reducing the need for constant human intervention. This shift toward greater intelligence and autonomy will unlock new possibilities for automation, improving efficiency and decision-making across industries while reshaping the way we live and work.

The Impact of AI on Small to Medium-Sized Businesses

Artificial Intelligence (AI) is no longer just a tool for large corporations with vast resources. Small to medium-sized businesses (SMBs) can also harness the power of AI to streamline operations, enhance customer experiences, and drive growth. This chapter delves into the transformative impact of AI on SMBs and provides actionable strategies for identifying relevant AI technologies and implementing them effectively.

1. Understanding the Impact of AI on SMBs

AI offers numerous benefits to SMBs, helping them compete with larger enterprises and navigate the complexities of the modern business landscape.

Key impacts include:

1.A. Enhanced Operational Efficiency

AI can automate routine tasks such as data entry, customer service inquiries, and inventory management. This frees up valuable time for employees to focus on strategic activities, reducing operational costs and increasing efficiency.

1.B. Improved Customer Experience

AI-powered tools like chatbots, personalized recommendations, and sentiment analysis enable SMBs to provide personalized and responsive customer service. This leads to higher customer satisfaction and loyalty.

1.C. Data-driven Decision-making

AI can analyze large volumes of data to uncover patterns and insights that inform business decisions. This helps SMBs make more accurate forecasts, optimize pricing strategies, and identify new market opportunities.

1.D. Competitive Advantage

By leveraging AI, SMBs can differentiate themselves from competitors through innovative products, services, and customer experiences. AI can level the playing field, allowing smaller businesses to compete with larger firms.

2. Strategies for Identifying Relevant AI Technologies

Implementing AI effectively requires a clear understanding of which technologies are relevant to your business needs.

Here are some strategies to help SMBs identify the right AI tools:

2.A. Assess Business Goals and Challenges

Begin by evaluating your business objectives and pain points. Identify areas where AI can provide the most value, such as improving customer service, increasing sales, or optimizing operations. This will help you focus on the AI technologies that align with your goals.

2.B. Research AI Solutions

Stay informed about the latest AI developments and solutions. Read industry reports, attend webinars, and follow AI thought leaders. Understanding the capabilities of different AI tools will help you make informed decisions.

2.C. Conduct a Needs Assessment

Evaluate your current processes and identify areas where AI can make a significant impact. Consider factors such as data availability, process complexity, and potential return on investment. This assessment will help you prioritize AI initiatives.

2.D. Consult with Experts

Engage with AI consultants or vendors who specialize in SMB solutions. They can provide valuable insights into the most suitable AI technologies for your business and help you navigate the implementation process.

2.E. Pilot Projects

Start with small-scale AI projects to test their effectiveness and feasibility. Pilots allow you to evaluate AI solutions in a controlled environment and gather data on their performance before committing to a full-scale implementation.

3. Implementing AI in SMBs: A Step-by-Step Guide

Once you have identified the relevant technologies, the next step is implementation.

Here's a step-by-step guide to help SMBs integrate AI into their processes:

3.A. Define Clear Objectives

Set specific, measurable goals for your AI initiatives. Whether it's customer response times, reducing customer response times, or increasing sales conversion rates, clear objectives will guide your implementation efforts and help you measure success.

3.B. Prepare Your Data

AI relies on high-quality data for training and operation. Ensure your data is clean, accurate, and well-organized. Implement data governance practices to maintain data quality and security.

3.C. Choose the Right AI Tools

Select AI tools that align with your business needs and technical capabilities. Consider factors such as ease of use, integration with existing systems, scalability, and vendor support. Tools like chatbots, predictive analytics, and machine learning platforms are popular choices for SMBs.

3.D. Build a Skilled Team

Assemble a team with the necessary skills to implement and manage AI solutions. This may include data scientists, IT professionals, and business analysts. Investing in training and development will ensure your team can effectively leverage AI technologies.

3.E. Integrate AI Tools

Integrate AI tools into business processes, workflows, and systems. This may involve customizing the AI solution to fit your specific needs and ensuring seamless data flow between systems. Collaboration between IT and business units creates a successful integration.

3.F. Monitor and Optimize

Continuously monitor the performance of your AI solutions. Collect feedback from users and analyze performance metrics to identify areas for improvement. Regularly update and refine your AI models to ensure they remain effective and relevant.

3.G. Scale and Expand

Once you have successfully implemented AI in one area of your business, look for opportunities to scale and expand. Apply the lessons learned from your initial projects to other parts of your organization. Scaling AI across the business can amplify its impact and drive greater value.

4. Overcoming Challenges in AI Implementation

Implementing AI in SMBs can be challenging, but these obstacles can be overcome with careful planning and execution.

4.A. Limited Resources

SMBs often have limited financial and human resources. To mitigate this, start with small, high-impact projects that require minimal investment. Leverage cloud-based AI solutions that offer flexible pricing models and reduce the need for extensive in-house infrastructure.

4.B. Data Privacy and Security

Protecting customer data is critical when implementing AI. Ensure compliance with data privacy regulations and implement robust security measures. Educate your team on data protection best practices to minimize risks.

4.C. Change Management

Introducing AI can disrupt existing workflows and face resistance from employees. Communicate the benefits of AI clearly and involve employees in the implementation process. Provide training and support to help them adapt to new technologies.

4.D. Skill Gaps

AI implementation requires specialized skills that may not be readily available in SMBs. Invest in training programs and consider partnering with external experts or vendors to bridge the skill gap.

5. Conclusion

The impact of AI on small to medium-sized businesses is profound. By automating processes, enhancing customer experiences, and enabling data-driven decision-making, AI can drive significant growth and competitive advantage. However, successful implementation requires careful planning, a clear understanding of relevant technologies, and a strategic approach.

SMBs can start their AI journey by assessing their business needs, conducting pilot projects, and gradually scaling their AI initiatives. With the right strategies and resources, SMBs can harness the power of AI to transform their operations and achieve sustainable growth in the digital age.

The Impact of AI on Physical In-Person Businesses

AI is revolutionizing not only the digital realm but also the landscape of physical, in-person businesses. From retail stores to restaurants, healthcare facilities, and manufacturing plants, AI is redefining how businesses operate. It's helping companies streamline processes, improve decision-making, and create more personalized and efficient customer experiences. As AI continues to evolve, its potential to reshape the way we interact with the physical world is becoming more apparent, making it an essential tool for businesses looking to stay competitive in today's rapidly changing market.

In industries like retail and hospitality, AI-powered tools are being used to optimize inventory management, personalize customer recommendations, and automate routine tasks, allowing employees to focus on more complex, value-added activities. In healthcare, AI is being integrated into diagnostic systems, improving patient outcomes by analyzing vast amounts of medical data to provide faster and more accurate results. Manufacturing plants are using AI for predictive maintenance, reducing downtime, and improving productivity by anticipating equipment failures before they happen. Across various sectors, the implementation of AI is leading to more streamlined operations, cost savings, and ultimately, business growth.

This chapter will explore the profound impact AI is having on physical businesses, offering a deep dive into how it can be successfully integrated across different industries. Through practical strategies and real-world examples, we'll examine how AI is transforming customer experiences and operational processes. As we move forward, you'll gain valuable insights into the key considerations and best practices for leveraging AI in your business, positioning you to harness its full potential.

1. Understanding the Impact of AI on Physical In-Person Businesses

AI offers a myriad of benefits to physical businesses by improving efficiency, customer satisfaction, and operational agility. Key impacts include:

1.A. Enhanced Customer Experience

AI-powered technologies like facial recognition, personalized recommendations, and automated checkout systems create seamless and personalized customer experiences, making in-person interactions more enjoyable and efficient.

1.B. Operational Efficiency

AI can optimize various operational aspects such as inventory management, supply chain logistics, and staff scheduling. This leads to reduced waste, improved productivity, and cost savings.

1.C. Predictive Maintenance

For businesses reliant on machinery and equipment, AI-driven predictive maintenance can foresee potential failures before they occur, reducing downtime and maintenance costs.

1.D. Enhanced Security

AI-driven surveillance systems and real-time monitoring can enhance security and safety within physical spaces, providing peace of mind to both businesses and customers.

2. Strategies for Identifying Relevant AI Technologies for Physical Businesses

Implementing AI effectively requires identifying the most relevant technologies for your specific business needs. Here are some strategies to help physical businesses pinpoint the right AI tools:

2.A. Evaluate Business Needs and Goals

Begin by understanding your business objectives and identifying key areas where AI can provide value. Whether it's improving customer service, streamlining operations, or enhancing security, having clear goals will help you focus on relevant AI applications.

2.B. Conduct Market Research

Stay informed about the latest AI developments and solutions tailored for physical businesses. Industry reports, case studies, and expert consultations can provide insights into which technologies are being successfully used by similar businesses.

2.C. Perform a Needs Assessment

Assess your current processes to identify areas where AI can be beneficial. Consider aspects such as customer interactions, operational workflows, and equipment management. This assessment will highlight potential AI use cases.

2.D. Pilot Testing

Start with small-scale AI projects to evaluate their effectiveness. Pilot tests allow you to gather data on performance and make adjustments before rolling out AI solutions on a larger scale.

3. Implementing AI in Physical In-Person Businesses: A Step-by-Step Guide

Once you have identified the relevant AI technologies, the next step is implementation. Here's a comprehensive guide to help physical businesses integrate AI effectively:

3.A. Define Clear Objectives

Set specific, measurable goals for your AI initiatives. Whether it's reducing wait times, optimizing inventory, or improving security, clear objectives will guide your implementation efforts and help you measure success.

3.B. Prepare Your Data AI

Systems rely on high-quality data for training and operation. Ensure that your data is clean, accurate, and well-organized. Implement robust data management practices to maintain data quality and security.

3.C. Choose the Right AI Tools

Select AI tools that align with your business needs and technical capabilities. Consider factors such as ease of use, integration with existing systems, scalability, and vendor support. Popular tools for physical businesses include:

- AI-driven POS systems
- Customer analytics platforms
- Security monitoring solutions

3.D. Build a Skilled Team

Assemble a team with the necessary skills to implement and manage AI solutions. This may include:

- Data scientists
- IT professionals
- Business analysts

Investing in training and development will ensure your team can effectively leverage AI technologies.

3.E. Integrate AI into Business Processes

Integrate AI tools into your existing workflows and systems. Customize the AI solutions to fit your specific needs and ensure seamless data flow between systems. Collaboration between IT and business units is crucial for successful integration.

3.F. Monitor and Optimize

Continuously monitor the performance of your AI solutions. Collect feedback from users and analyze performance metrics to identify areas for improvement. Regularly update and refine your AI models to ensure they remain effective and relevant.

3.G. Scale and Expand

Once you have successfully implemented AI in one area of your business, look for opportunities to scale and expand. Apply the lessons learned from your initial projects to other parts of your organization. Scaling AI across the business can amplify its impact and drive greater value.

4. Overcoming Challenges in AI Implementation

Businesses Implementing AI in physical businesses can be challenging, but these obstacles can be overcome with careful planning and execution. Here are some common challenges and how to address them:

4.A. Limited Resources

Physical businesses often have limited financial and human resources. To mitigate this, start with small, high-impact projects that require minimal investment. Leverage cloud-based AI solutions that offer flexible pricing models and reduce the need for extensive in-house infrastructure.

4.B. Data Privacy and Security

Protecting Customer and business data is critical when implementing AI. Ensure compliance with data privacy regulations and implement robust security measures. Educate your team on data protection best practices to minimize risks.

4.C. Change Management

Introducing AI can disrupt existing workflows and face resistance from employees. Communicate the benefits of AI clearly and involve employees n the implementation process. Provide training and support to help them adapt to new technologies.

4.D. Skill Gaps

AI implementation requires specialized skills that may not be readily available in physical businesses. Invest in training programs and consider partnering with external experts or vendors to bridge the skill gap.

5. Case Studies of AI Implementation in Physical Businesses

5.A. AI in Retail: Personalized Shopping Experiences

A clothing retailer implemented an AI-powered recommendation system in their stores. By analyzing customer purchase history and preferences, the system provided personalized product suggestions. This not only increased sales but also enhanced customer satisfaction and loyalty.

5.B. AI in Restaurants: Optimizing Operations

A fast-food chain used AI-driven predictive analytics to optimize inventory management and staff scheduling. This resulted in reduced food waste, lower labor costs, and improved customer service during peak hours.

5.C. AI in Healthcare: Enhancing Patient Care

A healthcare clinic implemented AI-powered diagnostic tools to assist doctors in identifying conditions more accurately and quickly. This improved patient outcomes and allowed the clinic to handle more appointments efficiently.

5.D. AI in Manufacturing: Predictive Maintenance

A manufacturing plant used AI to monitor equipment performance and predict maintenance needs. This proactive approach reduced equipment downtime, extended machinery lifespan, and lowered maintenance costs.

Conclusion

The impact of AI on physical, in-person businesses is transformative. By automating processes, enhancing customer experiences, and enabling data-driven decision-making, AI can drive significant growth and competitive advantage. However, successful implementation requires careful planning, a clear understanding of relevant technologies, and a strategic approach.

Physical businesses can start their AI journey by:

- Assessing their needs
- Conducting pilot projects
- Gradually scaling their AI initiatives

With the right strategies and resources, physical businesses can harness the power of AI to transform their operations and achieve sustainable growth in the digital age.

Module 5
AI in Strategic Business

AI in Strategic Business Decision-Making

Artificial Intelligence is rapidly transforming the landscape of business strategy. In an era characterized by constant change and uncertainty, the ability to make informed, data-driven decisions is paramount. AI provides businesses with the tools to analyze vast amounts of data, uncover hidden patterns, predict future trends, and optimize decision-making processes. This module explores how AI can be integrated into strategic business decision-making, offering a comprehensive guide to leveraging AI for competitive advantage, operational efficiency, and financial growth.

The transition from traditional decision-making to AI-driven strategies allows businesses to move beyond reactive measures, enabling them to anticipate and proactively address challenges and opportunities. By integrating AI into their strategic planning processes, businesses can enhance their ability to navigate the complexities of the modern market, ensuring sustained growth and resilience.

1. AI-Powered Strategic Planning

Predictive Analytics for Future Planning

Predictive analytics is a cornerstone of AI's value proposition in strategic planning. By analyzing historical and real-time data, AI can identify trends, correlations, and patterns that offer valuable insights into future market behavior. Predictive analytics helps businesses forecast demand, optimize supply chains, and develop marketing strategies that are aligned with anticipated consumer needs.

Deep Dive into Predictive Analytics

Predictive analytics involves several key components, including data collection, data cleaning, model building, and result interpretation. AI systems like machine learning algorithms analyze historical data to build predictive models, which are then used to forecast future outcomes. For instance, Coca-Cola's AI-driven predictive analytics system considers various data points—weather conditions, economic indicators, and past sales data—to predict product demand across different regions. This allows Coca-Cola to fine-tune its production schedules and distribution networks, minimizing waste and maximizing efficiency.

Example: Coca-Cola's Demand Forecasting

Coca-Cola has integrated AI into its demand forecasting processes to optimize production and distribution. By analyzing a combination of sales data, external market factors, and consumer behavior, Coca-Cola's AI system can predict demand variations with high accuracy. This has enabled the company to reduce overproduction, lower storage costs, and enhance its responsiveness to market changes.

Scenario Simulation and Risk Management

Risk management is critical to strategic decision-making, and AI's ability to simulate various scenarios is transforming how businesses approach risk assessment.

Detailed Examination of Scenario Simulation

AI scenario simulation models allow businesses to explore multiple outcomes based on different variables, providing a comprehensive understanding of potential risks and rewards. These models are particularly valuable in volatile industries where external factors such as regulatory changes, economic shifts, or supply chain disruptions can have significant impacts. They utilize a range of data inputs to simulate possible scenarios, enabling businesses to prepare contingency plans for various potential risks.

Example: Tesla's Supply Chain Resilience

Tesla has implemented AI-driven models to enhance the resilience of its supply chain. These models simulate various disruption scenarios, such as supplier failures, transportation delays, or raw material shortages. By understanding the potential impacts of these disruptions, Tesla can develop and implement strategies that reduce risk, such as diversifying its supplier base or building up strategic reserves of critical materials.

2. Enhancing Competitive Advantage with AI

Real-Time Market Maintaining a competitive edge in today's fast-paced business environment requires real-time insights into market trends, competitor activities, and consumer sentiment. AI-powered market intelligence tools provide businesses with the ability to monitor these factors continuously, enabling them to make quick and informed decisions that keep them ahead of the competition.

In-Depth Look at Real-Time Market Intelligence

Real-time market intelligence involves the continuous collection and analysis of data from various sources, including social media, news outlets, financial reports, and customer feedback. AI tools can process this data at scale, identifying emerging trends and potential threats in real time. For example, sentiment analysis tools powered by natural language processing (NLP) can gauge public opinion on a brand or product, allowing companies to adjust their strategies swiftly in response to changing consumer sentiment.

Netflix is a prime example of a company that leverages AI for real-time market intelligence. By continuously analyzing viewer data, Netflix can adapt its content offerings to meet the evolving preferences of its audience. This ability to respond quickly to market changes has been a key factor in Netflix's success in the highly competitive streaming industry.

Example: Netflix's Adaptive Content Strategy Netflix uses AI to analyze the viewing habits and preferences of its global audience. The platform's recommendation engine, powered by machine learning, continuously learns from user interactions, enabling Netflix to:

- Tailor its content offerings to individual preferences
- Enhance user experience
- Drive engagement and retention

This real-time adaptability gives Netflix a significant competitive advantage in the streaming market.

Optimizing Product Development

AI is revolutionizing product development by:

- Accelerating the design process
- Improving product quality
- Reducing time-to-market

By analyzing customer feedback, market trends, and emerging technologies, AI helps companies identify opportunities for innovation and improvement, ensuring that their products remain relevant and competitive.

Detailed Exploration of AI in Product Development

AI-driven tools in product development include:

- Generative design software
- Predictive analytics
- Simulation models

Example: General Motors' AI-Driven Design Process integrates AI into its vehicle design and testing phases. Using advanced simulations to predict how new models will perform in real-world conditions, GM can:

- Identify potential issues during the design phase
- Make necessary adjustments before building physical prototypes

This AI-driven approach accelerates the development process, reduces costs, and enhances the safety and performance of GM's vehicles.

3. AI in Operational Efficiency

Supply Chain and Logistics Optimization

Supply chain efficiency is a critical factor in business success, and AI offers powerful tools for optimizing logistics and supply chain management. AI-driven solutions can analyze vast amounts of data from global operations, identifying inefficiencies and optimizing processes to reduce costs and improve delivery times.

Comprehensive Analysis of AI in Supply Chain Optimization

AI applications in supply chain management include predictive analytics for demand forecasting, real-time tracking of shipments, and dynamic route optimization. Predictive analytics helps companies anticipate demand fluctuations, allowing them to adjust inventory levels and production schedules accordingly. Real-time tracking systems use AI to monitor shipments and optimize delivery routes, reducing delays and improving customer satisfaction.

Example:

DHL's Global Logistics Optimization – DHL employs AI-driven solutions to optimize its logistics network, from warehouse management to route planning. The company's AI systems analyze data from thousands of shipments daily, predicting the most efficient delivery routes and optimizing warehouse operations. This has resulted in faster deliveries, reduced operational costs, and higher customer satisfaction, solidifying DHL's position as a leader in the logistics industry.

Automation of Routine Business Processes

Automation is one of AI's most significant contributions to operational efficiency. By automating routine tasks, businesses can reduce the workload on human employees, allowing them to focus on more strategic initiatives. AI-driven automation is transforming industries such as finance, HR, and customer service.

Expanded Discussion on AI-Driven Automation

In finance, AI is used to automate processes such as invoice processing, fraud detection, and financial reporting. These AI systems can process vast amounts of data with greater speed and accuracy than human workers, reducing errors and ensuring compliance with regulatory standards. In HR, AI-driven platforms handle tasks such as resume screening, employee onboarding, and performance evaluations, improving efficiency and consistency in HR operations.

Example: JP Morgan Chase's COIN Platform – The COIN platform uses advanced AI algorithms to analyze complex legal documents, identifying key clauses and potential risks in seconds. This automation has transformed JP Morgan's legal processes, reducing the time required for contract analysis from several months to just a few seconds. The result is not only increased efficiency but also greater accuracy and reduced legal risks.

4. AI-Driven Financial Decision-Making

Investment and Portfolio Management

AI's impact on investment and portfolio management is profound, offering tools that analyze vast data sets, identify trends, and make predictions that guide investment strategies. AI-driven platforms provide asset managers with real-time insights, helping them make more informed decisions that balance risk and reward effectively.

In-Depth Exploration of AI in Investment Management

AI applications in investment management include algorithmic trading, risk assessment, and portfolio optimization. Algorithmic trading systems use AI to execute trades at optimal times based on real-time market data and predictive models. Risk assessment tools analyze various factors, such as market volatility and geopolitical events, to evaluate the potential risks associated with different investments. Portfolio optimization algorithms help asset managers allocate resources in a way that maximizes returns while minimizing risk.

Example: BlackRock's Aladdin Platform – Aladdin, BlackRock's AI-powered platform, revolutionizes investment management by analyzing risks and opportunities across global markets. The platform's machine learning algorithms predict market movements and optimize portfolio allocations, helping asset managers achieve better returns while managing risk effectively. This AI-driven approach has been instrumental in BlackRock's success as one of the world's largest asset managers.

Cost Optimization and Revenue Growth

AI plays a crucial role in identifying cost-saving opportunities and optimizing pricing strategies, directly impacting a company's profitability. By analyzing operational data, AI can identify inefficiencies and suggest cost-saving measures, while dynamic pricing models help businesses maximize revenue.

Detailed Analysis of AI in Cost Optimization

AI-driven cost optimization involves the continuous analysis of operational data to identify areas where resources can be used more efficiently. This includes optimizing energy consumption, reducing waste, and streamlining processes. AI can also enhance revenue growth through dynamic pricing models that adjust prices based on real-time demand, competition, and other market factors.

Walmart is a leader in using AI for dynamic pricing. The company's AI-driven pricing system continuously monitors market conditions, competitor prices, and customer behavior to adjust prices in real-time. This allows Walmart to remain competitive while maximizing sales and profit margins.

Example: Walmart's Dynamic Pricing Model

Walmart's AI-driven pricing system is a key component of its competitive strategy. By continuously analyzing market data and customer behavior, the system adjusts product prices in real-time to reflect current demand and competitive pressures. This dynamic pricing approach allows Walmart to maximize revenue while maintaining its reputation for offering competitive prices.

5. Building a Resilient Business with AI

Crisis Management and Recovery

The ability to anticipate and respond to crises is essential for building a resilient business. AI plays a vital role in crisis management by providing real-time data analysis and predictive insights that help businesses prepare for and recover from unexpected events.

Expanded Examination of AI in Crisis Management

AI-driven crisis management involves several key components, including predictive analytics, real-time monitoring, and automated response systems. Predictive analytics can identify potential crises before they occur, allowing businesses to take preemptive action. Real-time monitoring systems provide continuous updates on the status of the crisis, enabling businesses to respond quickly and effectively. Automated response systems can manage communications, allocate resources, and execute contingency plans, reducing the impact of the crisis on business operations.

During the COVID-19 pandemic, AI played a critical role in managing the global response. BlueDot, an AI-powered health monitoring platform, successfully predicted the outbreak and its potential spread by analyzing data from various sources, including news reports, airline ticketing data, and public health records. This early warning allowed organizations and governments to prepare more effectively, demonstrating the critical role AI can play in crisis management and recovery.

Example: BlueDot's Early Warning System for COVID-19

BlueDot's AI-driven platform was among the first to detect the COVID-19 outbreak, using machine learning to analyze vast amounts of data from around the world. By identifying patterns in news reports, airline ticketing data, and other sources, BlueDot predicted the spread of the virus weeks before official warnings were issued. This early detection allowed governments and organizations to take preemptive actions, showcasing the power of AI in crisis management.

Continuous Learning and Adaptation

AI's capacity for continuous learning enables businesses to adapt and evolve their strategies in response to changing conditions. Machine learning algorithms can analyze past performance, assess the effectiveness of decisions, and refine strategies over time, ensuring that businesses remain agile and responsive.

Comprehensive Analysis of AI in Continuous Learning

Continuous learning in AI involves the use of machine learning algorithms that adapt over time based on new data and feedback. This process allows AI systems to improve their performance and accuracy, making them more effective in supporting decision-making processes. In a business context, continuous learning ensures that strategies remain relevant and effective as market conditions evolve.

IBM Watson exemplifies the power of continuous learning in AI. In the healthcare industry, Watson uses machine learning to analyze patient data, medical research, and treatment outcomes, continuously refining its diagnostic and treatment recommendations. This adaptive approach ensures that Watson's recommendations are based on the most current and accurate information available.

Example: IBM Watson's Adaptive Learning in Healthcare

IBM Watson uses continuous learning to improve its diagnostic and treatment recommendations. By analyzing vast amounts of medical data and learning from each case, Watson continuously updates its knowledge base, ensuring that its recommendations are aligned with the latest medical research and best practices. This adaptive approach has made Watson a valuable tool for healthcare providers, enabling more accurate and personalized patient care.

6. Ethical and Responsible AI in Business Strategy

Balancing Innovation with Ethical Standards

Maintaining ethical standards is paramount as AI becomes more integrated into business operations. Businesses must ensure that their AI systems are transparent, fair, and aligned with their corporate values. This involves implementing AI governance frameworks that promote responsible use and mitigate the risks associated with AI.

In-Depth Discussion on Ethical AI

Ethical AI involves addressing issues such as bias, transparency, accountability, and fairness. Businesses must ensure that their AI systems do not perpetuate biases or discrimination and that the decision-making processes of AI systems are transparent and understandable. Additionally, businesses must establish clear accountability for AI-driven decisions, ensuring that they align with ethical standards and corporate values.

Example: Unilever is an example of a company that has successfully balanced innovation with ethical standards in its AI practices. The company uses AI to enhance its recruitment processes, focusing on objective criteria such as skills and qualifications. This approach minimizes the risk of bias and ensures that hiring decisions are fair and inclusive.

Unilever's Ethical AI Practices in Recruitment

Unilever uses AI-driven tools to screen job applicants, ensuring that hiring decisions are based on objective criteria such as skills, qualifications, and experience. This approach reduces the potential for bias in the recruitment process, promoting diversity and inclusion within the company. Unilever's commitment to ethical AI practices demonstrates how businesses can leverage AI for innovation while maintaining fairness.

AI Governance and Compliance

Establishing robust AI governance frameworks is essential for maintaining accountability and transparency in AI-driven decision-making. Businesses must implement policies and practices that ensure AI systems are used responsibly and comply with relevant regulations and ethical guidelines.

Expanded Analysis of AI Governance

AI governance involves establishing clear policies and procedures for the development, deployment, and monitoring of AI systems. This includes ensuring that AI systems are transparent, explainable, and accountable. Governance frameworks should also address issues such as data privacy, security, and compliance with regulations such as the General Data Protection Regulation (GDPR).

AI's role in GDPR compliance and data privacy management highlights the importance of robust governance frameworks. GDPR requires businesses to ensure that personal data is processed in a way that is lawful, transparent, and fair. AI systems must be designed and operated in compliance with these regulations, ensuring that personal data is protected and that individuals' rights are respected.

Example:

AI in GDPR Compliance and Data Privacy Management

AI plays a critical role in ensuring compliance with GDPR and other data privacy regulations. AI-driven systems can monitor data processing activities, identify potential breaches, and ensure that personal data is handled in accordance with regulatory requirements. By establishing robust governance frameworks, businesses can mitigate the risks associated with AI and build trust with their customers and stakeholders.

7. Future Trends in AI and Strategic Business Decision-Making

Emerging Technologies and Their Impact on Business Strategy

The future of AI in business strategy is shaped by emerging technologies such as quantum computing, advanced machine learning algorithms, and AI ethics. These technologies promise to revolutionize how businesses approach strategic planning, offering new tools for analyzing complex data sets, optimizing operations, and making ethical decisions.

Detailed Exploration of Emerging AI Technologies

Quantum computing is one of AI's most promising emerging technologies. By harnessing the power of quantum mechanics, quantum computers can process vast amounts of data at unprecedented speeds, enabling businesses to solve complex problems that are beyond classical computers' reach. This has significant implications for strategic decision-making, as quantum computing can enhance AI's ability to analyze data, model scenarios, and optimize strategies.

Advanced machine learning algorithms, including deep learning and reinforcement learning, are also driving the evolution of AI. These algorithms allow AI systems to learn and adapt in more sophisticated ways, improving their ability to make predictions, automate processes, and support decision-making. As these technologies continue to evolve, they will play an increasingly important role in shaping business strategy.

AI ethics is another critical area of focus for the future. As AI becomes more integrated into business operations, ethical considerations will become increasingly important. This includes ensuring that AI systems are transparent, accountable, and aligned with ethical standards. Businesses that prioritize AI ethics will be better positioned to build trust with their customers and stakeholders, ensuring the long-term success of their AI initiatives.

Preparing Your Business for AI Integration

To remain competitive, businesses must prepare for AI integration by investing in the necessary infrastructure, skills, and governance frameworks. This involves not only adopting AI technologies but also fostering a culture of innovation and continuous learning.

Comprehensive Guide to AI Integration

Preparing for AI integration involves several key steps:

1. **Invest in Infrastructure**

   Businesses must invest in the necessary infrastructure, including data storage, processing capabilities, and AI platforms. This also includes ensuring that IT systems are secure and capable of supporting AI applications.

2. **Develop Skills and Expertise**

   Businesses must develop the skills needed to implement and manage AI systems. This includes:

   o Training employees in AI technologies, data analysis, and ethical AI practices.

   o Hiring AI specialists or partnering with external AI providers to access the expertise required for successful AI integration.

3. **Establish Governance Frameworks**

Responsible AI use requires governance frameworks that ensure compliance with relevant regulations. This includes:

- o Developing policies and procedures for AI development, deployment, and monitoring.
- o Ensuring that AI systems are transparent, explainable, and accountable.

4. **Foster a Culture of Innovation**

Encouraging employees to embrace new technologies, experiment with AI applications, and continuously improve their skills is essential. A culture of innovation ensures businesses remain agile and responsive to the opportunities and challenges presented by AI.

AI in Strategic Decision-Making

The integration of AI into strategic decision-making marks a transformative shift in how businesses approach operations and long-term planning. AI enables:

- **Precision, Speed, and Data-Driven Insights**

  Companies can make more informed decisions based on real-time information and predictive analytics. This capability helps anticipate market trends, identify potential risks, and uncover new opportunities with greater accuracy.

- **Process Optimization and Enhanced Decision-Making**

By leveraging AI-driven automation and advanced data analysis, companies can build more efficient, agile, and responsive strategies that foster growth and innovation.

Looking Ahead: AI's Impact on Business Strategy

As AI continues to evolve, its influence on business strategy will become even more significant. Companies that embrace AI will be better equipped to:

- Navigate uncertainty and adapt to rapid market changes.
- Enhance operational efficiency.
- Improve customer experiences.
- Drive innovation across all aspects of business strategy.

In an increasingly competitive environment, the ability to leverage AI in strategic decision-making is becoming a crucial differentiator.

As AI continues to evolve, its impact on business strategy will become even more significant. Companies that embrace AI will be better equipped to navigate uncertainty and adapt to rapid changes in the market. From enhancing operational efficiency to improving customer experiences and driving innovation, AI's influence will permeate every aspect of business strategy.

Conclusion: Unlocking the Full Potential of AI

Artificial intelligence holds immense potential to transform industries, drive innovation, and improve lives. By embracing AI technologies and overcoming ethical challenges, we can unlock unprecedented possibilities and usher in a new era of progress and prosperity.

As we conclude this comprehensive guide on integrating artificial intelligence into business processes, it is clear that AI possesses the power to revolutionize industries, enhance operational efficiency, and drive innovation. By strategically implementing AI technologies, businesses can unlock new opportunities, gain a competitive edge, and achieve sustainable growth.

As you embark on your AI journey, remember to:

- **Prioritize ethical considerations**
- **Commit to continuous learning**
- **Manage data carefully**

Together, we can harness the transformative power of AI to build a more prosperous and better future.

Thank you for joining us on this exciting journey!

Nikhal Ghai and Nikky Kho

Real AI Dynamics

P.S. If you're interested in exploring our company's AI Bootcamps or online workshops to learn more about how AI can transform your business—or if you'd like to gain deeper insight into AI advancements and digital products—visit realaidynamics.com for more information.

ONE LAST MESSAGE

Unlock AI Mastery is a comprehensive guide aimed at helping businesses understand and implement artificial intelligence (AI) to drive innovation, efficiency, and competitiveness. Written by **Nikhal Ghai and Nikky Kho**, the e-book is structured to simplify complex AI concepts, making them accessible to both beginners and professionals looking to incorporate AI into their operations.

The book begins by outlining the potential of AI across various industries, showcasing real-world applications in sectors like healthcare, finance, manufacturing, and retail. These examples illustrate how AI can streamline operations, enhance customer experience, and create a competitive edge for businesses. The book covers how AI technologies transform core business functions like marketing, sales, and human resources, from AI-powered chatbots to predictive analytics. One of the key themes is the importance of integrating AI into business processes. The authors emphasize that successful AI adoption requires a well-defined strategy aligned with business objectives.

This involves selecting the right AI tools, configuring them according to the business needs, and continuously monitoring their performance to optimize results. The book provides practical steps for businesses to assess their readiness for AI, address skill gaps, and overcome challenges like data quality and organizational resistance.

Ethics and responsible AI use are critical factors for businesses to consider. The book addresses potential risks, such as bias in AI systems, privacy concerns, and the need for transparency and accountability. The authors encourage companies to establish ethical guidelines and governance frameworks to ensure the responsible use of AI technologies.

The guide also includes a roadmap for developing an AI-driven strategy, offering insights into how businesses can prioritize AI initiatives, measure success, and scale their AI efforts. The authors present real-world case studies showcasing how companies have leveraged AI to achieve significant improvements in efficiency, customer satisfaction, and revenue growth.

In conclusion:

Unlock AI Mastery provides a clear and actionable framework for companies looking to harness the power of AI. It emphasizes the importance of continuous learning, ethical considerations, and strategic alignment to unlock the full potential of AI technologies in driving business success.

Artificial intelligence holds immense potential to transform industries, drive innovation, and enhance operational efficiency.

By strategically implementing AI technologies, businesses can unlock unprecedented opportunities, achieve sustainable growth, and gain a competitive edge—all while navigating the ethical and data-driven challenges of the digital age.

We Have a Special FREE Bonus Gift for You

Kickstart your journey to mastering AI and understanding its vital role in shaping today's world.

Claim Your FREE Bonus Gift:

https://www.freegiftfromnikky.com

Acknowledgements

We would like to express our heartfelt gratitude to the amazing team at Real AI Dynamics, whose relentless dedication and innovation have been the driving force behind this project.

To Luan Carvalho, for helping us start this book.

Isiah Alcala, your creativity and insights have been instrumental in shaping our ideas and strategies, especially with the pioneering work on marketing at Real AI Dynamics.

Agnes Goh and Eric Jackson whose work saw us through the finish line for this book.

Ranju Ghai, your unwavering support for me (Nikhal) and belief in this mission have been a constant source of motivation.

A special thank you to the Real AI Dynamics team, whose expertise and passion have empowered our clients and played a crucial role in advancing the impact of AI in businesses worldwide. Your contributions are invaluable and deeply appreciated.

Special Mentions:

Abhiraj Tiwari, Alvin Lin, Andrew Kolarzh, Arnav Rage, Avanthi Sanjana, Avery Clark, Boao Chen, Braden Johnson, Bryon Jones, Calvin Tiamzon, Cameron Campbell, Cheshta Santosh, Deborah Ukaegbu, Deepika Kuntumalla, Dhanvanth

Sundar Sankar, Divyanshu Chadha, Dominic Aniebonam, Dubem Eric, Emily Pressman, Gaetan Rutayisire, Gideon Stott, Gina Schowe, Jay Nettles, Jerry Sa, Jonathan Bench, Julia Bahr, Justus Seeley, Kaleb Tsegaye, Kevin Ly, Kevyn Lopez, Krish Sav, Krishna Khandelwal, Kumari Akshay Karthik, Lana Kersanava, Luke Avil, Madiga Gillan Mubeem, Marvin Balmaceda, Megha Chand, Naman Modi, Nisrina Akalusyamoktika, Pavan Sai Pedapudi Ayush Srivastava, Prateek Pravanjan, Ricky Rivera, Rishab Singh, Shreyank Shivaprakash, Sibel Yilmaz, Sofia Requejado, Sophia Barron, Srinivas Aditya Kual, Sundar Sankar, Syed Shuvo, Tarunvidyut Ravisankar, and Yasmin Carvalho.

YPO Forum Support:

Jack Levy, Alex Howland, Andrew Klymenko, Marc Kielburger, and Laila Leonida.

RAID Instructors, Partners, and Mentors:

Brad Moss, Brenna Wilkinson, Britany Wang, Bryan Talebi, Chase Olson, Chris Mathews, Cory Warfield, Daniel Arita, Dima Kozlov, Dina Colada, Frank Devito, Hanson Robotics, Jeremiah Younoussi, Jia Chen, Jim Ross, John Cho, Jonathan Webster, Kang Dhang, Kyle Spencer, Lee Kara Friedlander, Lindsay Hadley, Luan Oak, Michael Citrin, Michaelle Abraham, Phil Neil, Robert Rex, Ryan Wenger, Stephen Sideroff, Stephen Steiner, and Zack Judson.

Sponsors, Hosts, and Organizations:

Adobe, AIJA, Banco Industrial, Brigham Young University, BYU Pathways, BYU-Hawaii, ChainXChange, City Gala, CNN, Culture Builders, Danube Properties, Entrepreneur, EO, Forbes, Harvard, Inc. Magazine, LAToken, Loyola Marymount University, LV Napoleon Hill Institute, Nasa, Silicon Slopes, Speakers Authors Networking Group (SANG), Summit Series, The Church of Jesus Christ of Latter-day Saints, The White House, Transamerica Financial Advisors, United Nations, Universidad del Valle de Guatemala, University of Utah, University of Wisconsin-Madison, USC, Utah Tech Week, Vjal Institute, Vistage, Volcano Summit, World Cryptocon, and YPO.

Inspiration and Collaborators:

Kevin Harrington, Bryan Tracy, Joe Theismann, James Malinchak, Adam Farfan, Aditya Paul Berlia, Al Pacino, Alsdo Schwarz, Amanda Homes, Amber Ostergaard, Andrew Anderson, Anthony Mackie, Anthony Melikhov, Ashton Kutcher, Big Mike, Bill Walsh, Bradley Cooper, Brandon Carter, Brianna Thaxton, Brock Pierce, Bryan Gerber, Bryan Post, Buzz Aldrin, Calio Platam, Carrie Baily, Chad Nicely, Charlize Theron, Chris Kai, Chris Madero, Dan Fleysham, Dan Noffsinger, Daven Michaels, David Hauser, DJ Jazzy Jeff, Dmitriy Kozlov, Drew Hollar, Elliot Hulse, Eva Longoria, Gary Chappell, Gary Vaynerchuk, Gene Lim, Greg O'Gallagher, Halley Berry, Harry Yeh, Harvey Mackay, Jack Dorsey, James

Adams, James Cameron, James Malinchak, James Swanwick, Jamil Apostol, Jason Hartman, Jaylen James, Jeff Hanson, Jenn Lim, Jim Kwik, Joe Sugarman, John Paul DeJoria, John Sykes, John Travolta, Johnny Depp, Jon Teo, Jose Laveaga, Justus Seeley, Kabir Rajput, Keith Ferrazzi, Kristen Van Wey, Lara Stein, Larry Benet, Les Brown, Lewis Howes, Lindsey Stirling, Luciano Singer, Marianne Tanada, Mario Lopez, Mark Cuban, Mathew McConaughey, Michael Berdkan, Michael Gerver, Mike Warren, Mohamed Moretta, Molly Bloom, Nadeem Kassam, Neal Sperling, Nick Cantarella, Nick Friedman, Owen Cook, Paris Hilton, Perry Belcher, President Bill Clinton, Prince Malik, Quincy Owens, Randy Jackson, Ray Kurzweil, Reid Hoffman, Rhona Bennett, Richard Branson, Richard Dreyfus, Rob Kosberg, Rocky Wang, Roger Love, Scott O'Neil, Sekou Andrews, Self Mastery Co., Sharath Cherian, Sophia, Stephen M.R. Covey, Steve Wozniak, Sylvester Stallone, Tai Lopez, Ted Turner, Tim Ferris, Todd Peterson, Tony Hsieh, Torin Pavia, Troy Gray, and TyDy.

About Nikky Kho

Nikky Kho is the #1 Serial Entrepreneur Mentor and Creator of the Best Global AI Tech Startup Houses. He has spoken at and hosted 10,000 presentations in 270 cities and 70 countries. His expertise in AI entrepreneurship makes him an in-demand speaker and consultant with fees ranging from $15,000 to $100,000. Over 1,000 media networks approached him for news, magazines, television, documentaries, and podcasts. Nikky is repeatedly featured as CEO of one of America's fastest-growing companies on the prestigious Inc. 5000 List.

Nikky served as a distinguished business lecturer at top institutions, including Stanford, Wharton, Harvard, USC, Loyola Marymount, University of Utah, BYU, and University of Wisconsin-Madison. His lectures draw on experience in entrepreneurship, venture management, and technology.

Nikky founded 80 businesses, is an Eagle Scout, 150-country traveler, a culinary-school-trained vegan chef, family office investor, climbed Mount Everest, completed Half Ironman Australia and Vegas Marathons, was church missionary for self-reliance & entrepreneurship education, and loves fine art & Pebble Beach golf.

Interested in learning more about Nikky Kho? Visit:

- https://www.nikkykho.com
- https://www.linkedin.com/in/nicholaskho

About Nikhal Ghai

Nikhal Ghai is a dynamic young entrepreneur who began building businesses at just 12 years old, showcasing an early passion for innovation and problem-solving. Over time, he founded his own AI agency, has worked startups, and helped established companies to harness the power of artificial intelligence. His work focuses on practical, real-world applications of AI that drive business growth and operational efficiency.

As Head of Operations and the Co-Founder of Real AI Dynamics, Nikhal leads day-to-day functions, optimizing processes and aligning teams with the company's strategic vision. His passion for AI and entrepreneurship has driven him to the forefront of the industry, where he continues to explore how AI can transform industries and improve lives. Through his leadership and expertise, he is committed to helping businesses leverage AI for innovation and long-term success.

You can connect with Nikhal at:

- https://www.linkedin.com/in/nikhalghai/
- https://www.nikhalghai.com

AI Tools

Real AI Dynamics AI Tools Directory

Updated August 14, 2024

Written Content Creation

AI Tool	Link	Description	Possible Use Cases
Jasper AI		AI content generation	Blog writing, marketing copy, creative content
Designrr		Content repurposing	Ebook creation, content marketing, lead generation
Tome		AI-powered storytelling tool that creates presentations	Designing interactive presentations, storytelling for branding, and automated slide generation.

Workflow Automation

AI Tool	Link	Description	Possible Use Cases
n8n		Workflow automation	Automating tasks, integrating apps, improving efficiency

Microsoft Power Automate		Workflow automation	Streamlining processes, automating repetitive tasks, data integration
Zapier		App integration automation	Connecting apps, automating workflows, streamlining processes
Circleback AI		Contact management	Networking, contact updates, business relationships

Audio and Video Content Creation Custom AI Chatbots

AI Tool	Link	Description	Possible Use Cases
Synthesia		AI video creation	Automating tasks, integrating apps, improving efficiency
Heygen		AI-generated avatars	Streamlining processes, automating repetitive tasks, data integration
Udio AI		Voice synthesis	Connecting apps, automating workflows, streamlining processes
Replica		AI voice actors	Networking, contact updates, business relationships

Wonderdynamics		AI for VFX	Visual effects, film production, animation
Dalle-3		AI image generation	Creating images, graphic design, visual content
Midjourney		AI art generation	Art creation, graphic design, creative projects
Pictory		AI video editing	Video creation, content marketing, social media videos
Capcut		Video editing software	Video editing, social media content, marketing videos
PlayHT		AI voice synthesis	Audio content creation, voiceovers, interactive voice applications
Fireflies AI		Video editing software	Meeting notes, action items, searchable transcriptions
Invideo AI		Meeting transcription	Video production, social media content, marketing videos

Tool	QR	Function	Use Cases
Fireflies AI		AI video creation (text to video)	Meeting notes, action items, searchable transcriptions
Veed.io		Online video editor	Video editing, social media content, marketing videos
Descript		Audio/video editing	Podcast editing, video production, transcription
Adobe Firecut		Video editing AI	Video production, editing automation, content creation
Adobe Photoshop		Image editing software	Photo editing, graphic design, creative content
Clipdrop.co Stable Diffusion 3		AI image generation	Creating images, design projects, visual content
Remini		Photo enhancement AI	Restoring photos, enhancing image quality, creative projects
Speechify		Text-to-speech	Accessibility, audio content, learning tools

Elevenlabs		Text-to-speech	Voiceovers, accessibility, virtual assistants
Adobe Firefly 3		AI-based generative tool for creating images, text effects, and graphic design assets.	Includes tools for text-to-image generation, inpainting, and image editing, integrated within Adobe Creative Cloud
Luma Labs		AI-powered 3D content creation tool for immersive experiences and visuals.	3D content creation, virtual environments, video game development.
ChatGPT		Conversational AI	Customer support, content creation, and AI research
Leia Pix		Transform images into video	Animate photos for marketing
Notebook LM		Podcast generator from text	Create audio podcast shows on your content
Kling AI		Text to video	Create video content

Custom AI Chatbots

AI Tool	Link	Description	Possible Use Cases
CustomGPT		Custom AI models	Personalized AI solutions, specific business applications
Poe		AI chatbots	Customer support, virtual assistants, automated responses
Pi.ai		Personal AI assistant	Task management, scheduling, personal productivity
CallAnnie		AI calling assistant	Customer support, virtual receptionist, appointment scheduling
Make		Workflow automation	Connecting apps, automating tasks, streamlining workflows
Character AI		Custom AI chatbots and avatars	Virtual customer support agents, interactive storytelling, personalized education bots
GPT-Trainer		Trains custom language models	Industry specific chat bots, personalize content generation, training model for specialized knowledge

Content Design and Enhancement

AI Tool	Link	Description	Possible Use Cases
Gamma		AI Presentations, websites and white papers	Generate instant powerpoint presentations, webpages, and content-based PDFs
Beautiful AI		AI presentation design	Creating visually appealing presentations, pitch decks
Magnific AI		AI-powered marketing	Marketing automation, personalized campaigns, customer insights
Slides AI		AI presentation assistant	Creating slides, enhancing presentations, and educational materials
Ideogram AI		Text-to-image generation	Visual content creation, marketing materials, educational tools
Poly AI		Conversational AI	Customer support, virtual assistants, interactive voice services
Krea		Creative AI tools	Art creation, design projects, creative content generation

Uizard		UI/UX design AI	Designing interfaces, prototyping, user experience enhancement
Usegalileo		AI-driven design	Graphic design, marketing materials, creative projects
Canva		Graphic design tool	Marketing materials, social media content, presentations
Glam		AI beauty filter	Social media content, photo enhancement, beauty industry
Taskade		Productivity tool	Task management, project collaboration, team productivity
Leonardo		Content Generation	AI-generated images for game art, graphic designing and branding assets, product design
Pika Labs		Text-to-image content	Stable Diffusion is often used for art, design, and content generation
Stable Diffusion		Text-to-image art creation	Graphic and marketing content design, visual storytelling, custom image creation

PowerMode AI		Idea generation, brainstorming, and refining concepts	Refining pitch decks, rapid prototyping, brainstorming and startup ideation and solutions
Artisse		Photo editing and transformation	Professional photo editing, social media enhancement, branding and marketing content
RunwayML		Text-to-video and video-to-video content generation	Create high quality video with unique effects, social media content, branded assets, instructional videos.

Specialized AI Tools

AI Tool	Link	Description	Possible Use Cases
Enhanced AI		AI middleware	Connect, execute, and automate available AI tools
Hugging Face		NLP and ML models	Natural language processing, machine learning, text analysis
Suno AI		Conversational AI	Chatbots, virtual assistants, customer support
Xano		Backend development	API development, database management, backend support
Groq		AI acceleration hardware	High-performance computing, AI model training, data processing
Weights and Biases		ML experiment tracking	Monitoring experiments, model tracking, collaborative research
Rewind.ai		AI memory assistant	Meeting summaries, task tracking, personal organization

Gemini		AI-powered analytics	Business insights, data analysis, predictive analytics
Deep Gram AI		Speech recognition	Transcription, accessibility, voice analysis
Otter.ai		AI transcription	Meeting notes, transcriptions, accessibility
Letzchat		Language Translation	Transcription, Subtitles, dynamic content translation, in person events translations, custom solutions.
ID-ME		Digital identity wallet	Prevents identity theft and protects your documents
Delphi		Designed for ethical decision-making and moral reasoning	Used in AI safety and responsible AI.
Perplexity		Search engine	Finds answers to questions you may have.
Octoparse		Web Scraping	No code data scraping

Mintbird		E-commerce and sales funnel platform	Shopping cart and sales funnel builder, managing e-commerce marketing campaigns, tracking sales and conversion performance
Letterman Ai		Ai powered email newsletter generator	Create instant high quality emails newsletter contentQuizforma
Quizforma		Survey and quizzes	Capture data from clients
Page Sprout		Ai powered analytics	Track websites traffic

Raid Resources

At Real AI Dynamics, we offer a wide range of AI-powered tools and services to help businesses harness the full potential of artificial intelligence. Whether you're looking to streamline operations, enhance customer engagement, or boost productivity, our tools are designed to provide practical, scalable solutions that drive success. Below is a list of resources to support your AI journey.

Real AI Dynamics

Learn From The International Gold Standard in Generative Artificial Intelligence Training for Entrepreneurs & Global Business Leaders

Visit: https://www.RealAIDynamics.com/

Hot Seat Superconference

Step into the future of business optimization at the RAID Hot Seat Superconference, a unique, full-day event designed to revolutionize the way you approach your operations. Dive deep into your business with the guidance of AI experts, leveraging the best AI tools to unlock new levels of productivity across marketing, sales, finance, and human resources.

Visit: https://raidhotseat.com

Advanced AI Digital

Discover the pinnacle of AI education with the Advanced AI Digital program, a meticulously designed online platform catering to the evolving needs of entrepreneurs and business leaders. This comprehensive program offers immersive content available based on the tier of service you select. Dive into a wealth of cutting-edge AI knowledge, from foundational principles to advanced applications.

Visit: https://advancedaidigital.com

High Tech Mentoring

RAID High Tech Mentoring is a six-week online coaching experience, set within a digital mastermind format. This unique approach combines the depth of personalized mentorship with the breadth of collective wisdom, enabling participants to navigate the complexities of AI with confidence. Each week, mentees are immersed in sessions by leading mentors.

Visit: https://hightechmentoring.com

AI Executive Coach Certification

The AI Executive Coach Certification Program is designed to merge leadership coaching with the power of AI. This program equips you with cutting-edge AI tools, methodologies, and data-driven insights to transform your coaching effectiveness and set you apart in the market. Ideal for seasoned executive coaches, HR professionals, and leaders aiming to leverage AI for growth, our curriculum offers comprehensive learning, hands-on experience, and a focus on ethical considerations.

Visit: https://aiexecutivecoachcertification.com

Tech Startup House Mastermind

Tech Startup House is a year-long journey of creating a new AI-driven entrepreneurial venture. The program is structured into 5 modules: Startup, Scaleup, Systems, Sustainability, and Success. Each module addresses a critical phase of business development, starting with rapid ideation to gaining clients in the Startup module. In Scaleup module, focus shifts to growing revenue, followed by the Systems module, which emphasizes integrating frameworks. The Sustainability module is dedicated to creation of processes. Success module focuses on performance management to evaluate & amplify.

Visit: https://techstartuphousemastermind.com

AI App Lab

AI AppLab is a high technology implementation services combined with world-class AI education. Our AI App Design and Integration Services specialize in creating custom business apps, designed, and developed by a collaborative team of business strategists and technologists. Focused on enhancing operational processes, our AI-driven solutions streamline workflows, boost efficiency, and spur growth, ensuring your business stays ahead in the digital arena.

Visit: https://raidaiapplab.com

Immersion Training

RAID Immersion is a long-term, in-house artificial intelligence education, designed for organizations seeking to integrate AI capabilities. Tailored for weekly or monthly in-person sessions, this program is structured to foster AI training over an extended period. The immersive nature of the program ensures that learning is directly applicable, with hands-on workshops, collaborative projects, and case studies led by industry veterans.

Visit: https://raidimmersion.com

Whyai by Nikky Kho

Stay ahead of the curve with Nikky Kho, your go-to newsletter for the latest on AI bots and automation technology.

Visit: https://nikkyrecommends.com/newsletter

RAID Bootcamp: Elevate Your Business with AI

The RAID Bootcamp is a transformative 3-day program designed specifically for business leaders seeking to integrate artificial intelligence into their operations. This immersive experience provides a strategic foundation for using AI to enhance decision-making, streamline operations, and unlock new growth opportunities. By focusing on practical applications, the RAID Bootcamp ensures that AI becomes a tangible asset in driving your company's success.

Why Choose the RAID Bootcamp?

- **Strategic AI Implementation:** Our expert instructors collaborate with your team to implement tailored AI solutions that align with your specific business objectives, delivering immediate and measurable outcomes.

- **Live, Real-World AI Demonstrations:** Gain direct exposure to AI technologies that enhance operational efficiency, customer engagement, and data-driven decision-making. You'll see firsthand how AI can optimize your workflows and processes.

- **Custom, Business-Focused Learning:** The RAID Bootcamp is structured around your organization's unique needs, ensuring that you walk away with actionable insights and practical tools to lead AI-driven initiatives within your company.

The Competitive Advantage

In a rapidly evolving marketplace, the ability to effectively harness AI is a critical differentiator. The RAID Bootcamp positions you to lead your organization through the next phase of digital transformation, ensuring that AI becomes a driver of innovation and sustainable growth.

- **Duration:** 3 days
- **Format:** On-site or virtual options available
- **Enroll Now:** https://www.raidbootcamp.com

Made in the USA
Coppell, TX
14 December 2024

42538886R00085